ALFRED TENNYSON.

From a daguerreotype taken at the age of eighteen.

The Academy Classics

TENNYSON

IDYLLS OF THE KING

THE COMING OF ARTHUR   LANCELOT AND ELAINE

GARETH AND LYNETTE   THE HOLY GRAIL

THE PASSING OF ARTHUR

WITH INTRODUCTION AND NOTES BY

H. W. BOYNTON

———o⊙〉⊛〈⊙o———

1946

ALLYN AND BACON

BOSTON   NEW YORK   CHICAGO
ATLANTA   SAN FRANCISCO

COPYRIGHT, 1923
BY ALLYN AND BACON

REP

Norwood Press
J. S. Cushing Co. — Berwick & Smith Co.
Norwood, Mass., U.S.A.

PREFACE.

THIS edition of the *Idylls of the King* has been prepared to give in compact and convenient form the essential substance of the famous cycle, and such introductory and explanatory matter as is needed to make the poems intelligible without the use of other books of reference. In studying a piece of literature of this kind, rooted as it is in the past, there is no end to the amount of collateral and illuminative reading that may be profitably done. But few preparatory schools are in a position as to either time or equipment to prescribe very much of this kind of reading outside the class room.

The one book the present editor would like to see in the hands of every student of the Tennysonian *Idylls* would be our American classic, *The Boys' King Arthur* of Sidney Lanier — an admirable abridgment of the *Morte Darthur* of Sir Thomas Malory. Malory's narrative itself is too long for general reading. But there is no doubt that Tennyson knew it thoroughly, and that from a reading of it while he was still a very young man, he was moved to give his own poetic treatment of the Arthurian story.

In view of this very close relation between Tennyson's work and Malory's, the Notes of this edition embody a good deal of quotation from the *Morte Darthur*, so that the student may compare for himself the substance and savor of the two works, — the one written in the fifteenth century and the other in the nineteenth.

A word about the make-up of the text in this book. The colleges require the study of only four of the *Idylls*. In an earlier edition, I included only *The Coming of Arthur, Gareth and Lynette, Lancelot and Elaine,* and *The Passing of Arthur.* These seemed the indispensable four, if only four were to be read. But in using the book I felt a lack in the omission of *The Holy Grail,* since this poem sums up the mystical faith which was as much a part of the age of chivalry as its adventurous bravery. This *Idyll* is therefore included in the present edition, with Notes which should make plain the meaning of a poem in the nature of its theme somewhat more difficult than the simpler narratives of the four other *Idylls.*

H. W. Boynton.

In response to a suggestion, persuasively expressed, the oath of knighthood, from *Guinevere,* has been added at the end of the *Idylls.*

January, 1933.

CONTENTS.

————◆◆◆————

LIST OF ILLUSTRATIONS.

———◆◇◆———

INTRODUCTION.

LIFE OF TENNYSON.

ALFRED TENNYSON was born in the little village of Som-
ersby, Lincolnshire, on August 6th, 1809. His father, the
Reverend George Tennyson, was rector of this and two
other small parishes. He was a man of scholarly tastes,
and a great lover of good books. The mother of the family
was a clergyman's daughter. These lines in *The Princess*
are supposed to describe her :

> Not learned, save in gracious household ways,
> Not perfect, nay, but full of tender wants,
> No angel, but a dearer being, all dipt
> In angel instincts.

There were twelve children; Alfred was the third of the
seven boys. He was on close terms with his sister Emily,
and with his two older brothers; Charles, who was nearest in age, was his particular chum. They both began writing
very young. At eleven, Alfred had written a long epic poem in
imitation of Sir Walter Scott. At fourteen he had attempted
a poetic drama. Meanwhile he read everything good that he
could get hold of. After some elementary work in local
schools, the boys were prepared by their father for the university. In 1826 a local village bookseller printed *Poems
by Two Brothers*, a little volume made up of the verses of
Alfred and Charles Tennyson. They were good boyish
verses and not much more. Intimate as the brothers
were, they differed widely in temperament. Charles was

open-hearted, merry, and fond of company; Alfred was reserved, absent-minded, and liked to be much alone.

In 1828 they went together to Trinity College, Cambridge, where their older brother, Frederick, had preceded them a year or two earlier. Here Tennyson became intimate with Richard Monckton Milnes (afterwards Lord Houghton) and Arthur Henry Hallam, his closest friend in later years. It was Hallam whose death inspired the great elegy, "In Memoriam." Tennyson wrote a prize poem while at Cambridge; but it was the usual kind of thing. His real poetic work was the composition of most of the poems that appeared in 1830 under the title *Poems, Chiefly Lyrical.* Many of these verses had a new music in them, and so good a critic as Coleridge found praise for them. In 1831 Tennyson's father died, and the young poet left the university without taking his degree. In 1833 his second book of poems came out, *Poems, by Alfred Tennyson.* This volume showed a good deal of range, from classical themes like *Œnone* to British legend as in *The Lady of Shalott* (his first poetic experiment in the direction of the *Idylls of the King*), and from this to poems of the England of Tennyson's youth, like *The May Queen* and *The Miller's Daughter.* "More dewy, fresh, pathetic native verse has not been written since the era of *As You Like It* and *A Winter's Tale,*" says Edmund Clarence Stedman.

The volume contained much better poetry than the earlier one; but it was attacked and ridiculed by the intolerant critics of the day, who had not long before embittered the last years of Keats, and who were always ready to condemn anything that had a new form or a new savor. For ten years thereafter, Tennyson published nothing, which was probably as well for his work in the long run. Tennyson did not enjoy the mocking sort of criticism he had received, but he undoubtedly profited by it. Something of his long silence may have been owing also to the death of Hallam in the same year (1833) in which the poet underwent this first rough discipline at the hands of the critics. *In Memoriam,* the record of his friendship and his grief, was not published till 1850. Tennyson never made another friendship of the same quality and intensity. But when, about 1831, he went to live in London, he became on more than ordinarily friendly terms with some of the strongest men of his time, men like Walter Savage Landor, John Stuart Mill, William Makepeace Thackeray, and Thomas Carlyle. Perhaps his best portrait has been painted by Carlyle:

"A great shock of rough, dusty-dark hair; bright, laughing hazel eyes; massive, aquiline face, most massive, yet most delicate; of sallow brown complexion, almost Indian-looking; clothes, cynically loose, free and easy; smokes infinite tobacco. His voice is musically metallic — fit for loud laughter and piercing wail, and all that may lie between; speech and speculation free and plenteous. I do not meet, in these late decades, such company over a pipe."

Tennyson's mature fame began with the appearance in 1842 of the two-volume *"Poems of Alfred Tennyson."* He was now very favorably received by critics and public in both England and America. The very reviewers who ten years earlier had taken so harsh a tone now awarded to the still young writer a high place among English poets. Poe and Emerson in America were warm in their commendation. There were several reasons for this change in Tennyson's reception by his public. The 1833 poems were too novel in flavor to make their way at once. But during the ten years that followed, though he published nothing new, the

poet continued to be heard. The poems continued to be
read, to make their way against precedent and so gradually
to form a precedent of their own. In 1842 the volume of
reprinted verse was almost as warmly greeted as the volume
of later work. From now on Tennyson was to be the
mouthpiece of the dominant English mood. His earliest
work had come too soon. Both in matter and in form it
was strange to the taste of the hour. Henceforth he was
to be widely popular because always the spokesman of his age.

By 1845 he was so well-recognized a British institution as
to be granted a royal pension. In 1847 appeared *The Princess.*
The year 1850 saw the publication of *In Memoriam,* Tennyson's marriage to Emily Sellwood, and his appointment as
poet laureate of England. The most notable product of
the next five years was *Maud: a Monodrama.* This was
the poem which Tennyson, a famous reader, liked best to
read aloud to his friends, and all those who so heard it
hailed its beauty and power.

Meanwhile his poems of modern life did not divert him
from his old interest in epic or idyllic forms. The "idyll"
treatment of the Arthurian legends retained its charm for
him during more than half a century. Therefore the issue
in 1859 of the first four *Idylls of the King* simply fulfilled
the early promise of *The Lady of Shalott* and *Morte d'Arthur*
(1842); and the series was completed only with the pro-
duction of *Balin and Balan,* in 1885.

Apart from the work which centred in the completion of
this Arthurian cycle, his later years were given mainly to
two kinds of composition: the writing of modern domestic
idylls, like *Enoch Arden* and *Dora* and *Audley Court;* and
the experiments in poetic drama of which the best examples
were *Becket, The Cup,* and *Harold.* Tennyson was not by

nature a dramatist. His poetic plays show strong Shake-spearian influence in manner, and were the product of hard labor rather than inspiration. With *Becket* and *The Cup* the great actor Henry Irving had a good deal of success. But Tennyson was primarily a lyric poet. Some of his latest poems show still much of the singing magic which belonged to the first utterances of his youth.

The British custom of rewarding remarkable achievement in any field with a title, led to the offer of a baronetcy to Alfred Tennyson. This he declined, but later accepted a peerage, under the title "Baron Tennyson of Aldworth and Farringford." His later life was calm and cheerful, and he died, full of years and honors, on October 6th, 1892.

THE IDYLLS OF THE KING.

It is not known how early the legends of Arthur began to take form, nor how much foundation they had in fact. We first hear of them in Brittany, where, as they were passed down from generation to generation of Celts, they retained a pretty simple form. Arthur, the story ran, was a brave British king, who had a hand in the expulsion of the last Romans from Britain, and ruled wisely thereafter for many years. After the Norman Conquest of England, these legends were brought from Brittany to Wales, where they became common property. In 1147, Geoffrey of Monmouth, a Welsh priest in the court of Henry I, included the substance of them, with additions of his own, in his Latin prose *History of the Kings of Britain.* Wace, a Norman *trouveur,* rendered the legend in Norman French soon after; and from his narrative Layamon, a Saxon priest, transferred it to English verse. The situation is strange and suggestive: a Saxon tells, in the alliterative verse of his Teutonic inheritance, a story of the ancient Britons, which he has heard from a Norman, who gained it from a Latin work by a Welshman. Of such racial interweaving the fabric of modern English literature is made.

Another notable writer of Layamon's period also illustrates the composite character of English blood and English letters in that day. William of Malmesbury was son of a Norman father and a Saxon mother. Like many other writers of his century, he produced various narratives in Latin dealing with English history. One of them is of more than ordinary interest, as it suggests the germ of an idea which was about to possess the imagination of a whole race of singers and sayers: The Story of the Grail. According to this story, Joseph of Arimathea, in the course of his wanderings, had founded at Glastonbury the first church in England. With him was brought the Grail, the mystic vessel which had been used at the Last Supper, and in which the blood of Christ had been caught. Now, it chanced that, according to tradition, Joseph of Arimathea and King Arthur were both buried at Glastonbury; and it may have been this coincidence which, working upon the imagination of another ecclesiastic, Walter Map, linked the name of Arthur to the story of the Grail. The result was a romance in Norman French prose, called *The Quest of the Grail.*

To understand the amazing influence which the Grail legend had upon subsequent English poetry and prose, we must take it not as a chance product of the fancy, but as embodying the spirit of an age. During the twelfth century Europe was shaken by two great passions: for religion and for chivalry. The Norman had no match in his devotion to either of these passions; no wonder that he found an outlet for them both in that form of religious adventure, the Crusade. It is the crusading spirit in its purest form — the dream of gaining an ideal by hard blows — which animates the story of Walter Map. The same spirit produced in France the *Chansons de Geste,* dealing with Charlemagne; and in Spain, *The Cid.*

From such sources Sir Thomas Malory derived his version of the Arthurian story, *Le Morte Darthur;* it was written in the fifteenth century and printed by Caxton. This really great prose narrative, which has been reprinted several times of late, gained in its own day a very wide reading. Mainly from Malory, Tennyson drew the materials for the *Idylls;* but he employed these materials very differently. King Arthur, for instance, becomes in Tennyson a theoretically perfect creature, whose failure is due to adverse circumstances; while in Malory he is an heroic but fallible human being, who is in the end undone by the consequence of his own half-forgotten sin. Tennyson has, in short, simply selected and adapted such elements of the legend as he could employ in expressing his creed of modern idealism.

His method of developing the theme was extraordinary. *The Lady of Shalott,* a prefiguring of the story of *Elaine,* was written as early as 1832; the brief poems, *Sir Galahad, Sir Lancelot and Guinevere,* and *Morte d'Arthur,* appeared ten years later. *Morte d'Arthur* gave the first suggestion of epical treatment, and the substance of it was embodied in *The Passing of Arthur,* in the final version of the *Idylls.* The list of poems composing that complete version is worth giving, as there are many incomplete editions to be had. They are prefaced in the English edition by a dedication to the memory of Prince Albert, and followed by an address to Queen Victoria. Of the *Idylls* proper there are twelve: —

(1) The Coming of Arthur.
(2) Gareth and Lynette.
(3) The Marriage of Geraint.
(4) Geraint and Enid.
(5) Balin and Balan.
(6) Merlin and Vivien.
(7) Lancelot and Elaine.
(8) The Holy Grail.
(9) Pelleas and Ettarre.

(10) The Last Tournament.
(11) Guinevere.
(12) The Passing of Arthur.

In this order, as they are now printed, they constitute a fairly well-connected series of legends dealing with Arthur. They were, however, written at irregular intervals, extending altogether over a span of about twenty-seven years. In 1859 appeared a volume called *Idylls of the King,* containing what are now the third, fourth, sixth, seventh, and eleventh idylls. In 1870 appeared the first, eighth, ninth, and twelfth. Two years later appeared the second and tenth parts, and in 1885 appeared the fifth part. It is, as Henry van Dyke has remarked, an odd thing " that he should begin with the end, and continue with the beginning, and end with the middle of the story"; but the detached character of the parts, each complete in itself, made this manner of development not unnatural.

Many attempts have been made to treat the completed group of Idylls as if they actually made up a solid unit, — a great epic, in the sense that the *Æneid* and the *Odyssey* are great epics. There is no doubt that Tennyson had hoped to achieve something of the kind. From his earliest knowledge of the Arthurian legend, gained from a chance reading of Malory's *Morte Darthur,* he had dreamed of giving it an epical treatment on the highest plane. But his actual achievement is not a unified narrative. It is a series of elaborate sketches, more or less closely linked. As finally left, it possesses a sort of completeness; but not the completeness of a massive work consistently wrought according to a foregone plan.

The manner of composition was, as we have seen, irregular

and almost haphazard. The poet's ideas changed as he went on, both as to the meaning of the Arthurian story and as to its conduct. It is easy to point out minor inconsistencies in the final narrative, if we try to consider it as a whole. But we may better take them for granted as inevitable in a work composed in such fashion. We had better be content with the splendid pictures and episodes which fill the tales, instead of trying to wring from them a consistent plot or philosophy. They are unique and even great in their own way.

In the Notes to this edition of the five most important *Idylls*, frequent quotations are made from Malory. This is not done because *Le Morte Darthur* is historically accurate, but because it is incomparably the greatest of the earlier versions of the Arthurian story; and because it was the direct source from which Tennyson drew most of his materials. As will be seen, he made sometimes a close, oftener a very free, use of them. The quoted passages follow the modernized spelling of the Temple Edition of *Le Morte Darthur*. Malory's original narrative is too long and rambling for the general reader; but America has a Malory classic of its own, in the abridged *Boy's King Arthur* of the poet Sidney Lanier. It is a book full of glamour, and ought to be dipped into, at least, by all students of Tennyson's *Idylls*.

H. W. BOYNTON

TENNYSON IN HIS PRIME

IDYLLS OF THE KING.

THE COMING OF ARTHUR.

LEODOGRAN, the King of Cameliard,
Had one fair daughter, and none other child;
And she was fairest of all flesh on earth,
Guinevere, and in her his one delight.

For many a petty king ere Arthur came   5
Ruled in this isle, and ever waging war
Each upon other, wasted all the land;
And still from time to time the heathen host
Swarm'd overseas, and harried what was left.
And so there grew great tracts of wilderness,   10
Wherein the beast was ever more and more,
But man was less and less, till Arthur came.
For first Aurelius lived and fought and died,
And after him King Uther fought and died,
But either fail'd to make the kingdom one.   15
And after these King Arthur for a space,
And thro' the puissance of his Table Round,
Drew all their petty princedoms under him,
Their king and head, and made a realm, and reign'd

And thus the and of Cameliard was waste,   20
Thick with wet woods, and many a beast therein,
And none or few to scare or chase the beast;
So that wild dog, and wolf and boar and bear

Came night and day, and rooted in the fields,
And wallow'd in the gardens of the King.   20
And ever and anon the wolf would steal
The children and devour, but now and then,
Her own brood lost or dead, lent her fierce teat
To human sucklings; and the children, housed
In her foul den, there at their meat would growl,   30
And mock their foster-mother on four feet,
Till, straighten'd, they grew up to wolf-like men,
Worse than the wolves. And King Leodogran
Groan'd for the Roman legions here again,
And Cæsar's eagle : then his brother king,   35
Urien, assail'd him : last a heathen horde,
Reddening the sun with smoke and earth with blood,
And on the spike that split the mother's heart
Spitting the child, brake on him, till, amazed,
He knew not whither he should turn for aid.   40

But — for he heard of Arthur newly crown'd,
Tho' not without an uproar made by those
Who cried, ' He is not Uther's son ' — the King
Sent to him, saying, ' Arise, and help us thou !
For here between the man and beast we die.'   45

And Arthur yet had done no deed of arms,
But heard the call, and came : and Guinevere
Stood by the castle walls to watch him pass ;
But since he neither wore on helm or shield
The golden symbol of his kinglihood,   .   50
But rode a simple knight among his knights,
And many of these in richer arms than he,
She saw him not, or mark'd not, if she saw,
One among many, tho' his face was bare.

But Arthur, looking downward as he pass'd,   55
Felt the light of her eyes into his life
Smite on the sudden, yet rode on, and pitch'd
His tents beside the forest. Then he drave
The heathen; after, slew the beast, and fell'd
The forest, letting in the sun, and made   60
Broad pathways for the hunter and the knight,
And so return'd.

            For while he linger'd there,
A doubt that ever smoulder'd in the hearts
Of those great Lords and Barons of his realm
Flash'd forth and into war : for most of these,   65
Colleaguing with a score of petty kings,
Made head against him, crying, ' Who is he
That he should rule us ? who hath proven him
King Uther's son ? for lo ! we look at him,
And find nor face nor bearing, limbs nor voice,   70
Are like to those of Uther whom we knew.
This is the son of Gorloïs, not the King ;
This is the son of Anton, not the King.'

And Arthur, passing thence to battle, felt
Travail, and throes and agonies of the life,   75
Desiring to be join'd with Guinevere ;
And thinking as he rode, ' Her father said
That there between the man and beast they die.
Shall I not lift her from this land of beasts
Up to my throne, and side by side with me ?   80
What happiness to reign a lonely king,
Vex'd — O ye stars that shudder over me,
O earth that soundest hollow under me,
Vext with waste dreams ? for saving I be join'd

To her that is the fairest under heaven,   85
I seem as nothing in the mighty world,
And cannot will my will, nor work my work
Wholly, nor make myself in mine own realm
Victor and lord.   But were I join'd with her,
Then might we live together as one life,   90
And reigning with one will in everything
Have power on this dark land to lighten it,
And power on this dead world to make it live

    Thereafter — as he speaks who tells the tale —
When Arthur reach'd a field-of-battle bright   95
With pitch'd pavilions of his foe, the world
Was all so clear about him, that he saw
The smallest rock far on the faintest hill,
And even in high day the morning star.
So when the King had set his banner broad,   100
At once from either side, with trumpet-blast,
And shouts, and clarions shrilling unto blood,
The long-lanced battle let their horses run.
And now the Barons and the kings prevail'd,
And now the King, as here and there that war   105
Went swaying; but the Powers who walk the world
Made lightnings and great thunders over him,
And dazed all eyes, till Arthur by main might,
And mightier of his hands with every blow,
And leading all his knighthood, threw the Kings   110
Carados, Urien, Cradlemont of Wales,
Claudias, and Clariance of Northumberland,
The King Brandagoras of Latangor,
With Anguisant of Erin, Morganore,
And Lot of Orkney.   Then, before a voice   115
As dreadful as the shout of one who sees

To one who sins, and deems himself alone
And all the world asleep, they swerved and brake
Flying, and Arthur call'd to stay the brands
That hack'd among the flyers, 'Ho! they yield!'   120
So like a painted battle the war stood
Silenced, the living quiet as the dead,
And in the heart of Arthur joy was lord.
He laugh'd upon his warrior whom he loved
And honor'd most.   'Thou dost not doubt me King,   125
So well thine arm hath wrought for me to-day.'
'Sir and my liege,' he cried, 'the fire of God
Descends upon thee in the battle-field ;
I know thee for my King!'   Whereat the two,
For each had warded either in the fight,   130
Sware on the field of death a deathless love.
And Arthur said, 'Man's word is God in man:
Let chance what will, I trust thee to the death.'

Then quickly from the foughten field he sent
Ulfius, and Brastias, and Bedivere,   135
His new-made knights, to King Leodogran,
Saying, 'If I in aught have served thee well,
Give me thy daughter Guinevere to wife.'

Whom when he heard, Leodogran in heart
Debating — 'How should I that am a king,   140
However much he holp me at my need,
Give my one daughter saving to a king,
And a king's son ?' — lifted his voice, and call'd
A hoary man, his chamberlain, to whom
He trusted all things, and of him required   145
His counsel : 'Knowest thou aught of Arthur's birth ?'

Then spake the hoary chamberlain and said,
'Sir King, there be but two old men that know:
And each is twice as old as I; and one
Is Merlin, the wise man that ever served   150
King Uther thro' his magic art; and one
Is Merlin's master (so they call him) Bleys,
Who taught him magic; but the scholar ran
Before the master, and so far, that Bleys
Laid magic by, and sat him down, and wrote   155
All things and whatsoever Merlin did
In one great annal-book, where after-years
Will learn the secret of our Arthur's birth.'

To whom the King Leodogran replied,
'O friend, had I been holpen half as well   160
By this King Arthur as by thee to-day,
Then beast and man had had their share of me:
But summon here before us yet once more
Ulfius, and Brastias, and Bedivere.'

Then, when they came before him, the King said, 165
'I have seen the cuckoo chased by lesser fowl,
And reason in the chase; but wherefore now
Do these your lords stir up the heat of war,
Some calling Arthur born of Gorloïs,
Others of Anton?   Tell me, ye yourselves,   170
Hold ye this Arthur for King Uther's son?'

And Ulfius and Brastias answer'd, 'Ay.'
Then Bedivere, the first of all his knights
Knighted by Arthur at his crowning, spake —
For bold in heart and act and word was he,   175
Whenever slander breathed against the King —

'Sir, there be many rumors on this head:
For there be those who hate him in their hearts,
Call·him baseborn, and since his ways are sweet,
And theirs are bestial, hold him less than man,   180
And there be those who deem him more than man,
And dream he dropp'd from heaven; but my belief
In all this matter — so ye care to learn —
Sir, for ye know that in King Uther's time
The prince and warrior Gorloïs, he that held   185
Tintagil castle by the Cornish sea,
Was wedded with a winsome wife, Ygerne:
And daughters had she borne him, — one whereof,
Lot's wife, the Queen of Orkney, Bellicent,
Hath ever like a royal sister cleaved   190
To Arthur, — but a son she had not borne.
And Uther cast upon her eyes of love:
But she, a stainless wife to Gorloïs,
So loathed the bright dishonor of his love,
That Gorloïs and King Uther went to war: 195
And overthrown was Gorloïs and slain.
Then Uther in his wrath and heat besieged
Ygerne within Tintagil, where her men,
Seeing the mighty swarm about their walls,
Left her and fled, and Uther enter'd in,   200
And there was none to call to but himself.
So compass'd by the power of the King,
Enforced she was to wed him in her tears,
And with a shameful swiftness : afterward,
Not many moons, King Uther died himself,   205
Moaning and wailing for an heir to rule
After him, lest the realm should go to wrack.
And that same night, the night of the new year,
By reason of the bitterness and grief

That vex'd his mother, all before his time   210
Was Arthur born, and all as soon as born
Deliver'd at a secret postern-gate
To Merlin, to be holden far apart
Until his hour should come; because the lords
Of that fierce day were as the lords of this,   215
Wild beasts, and surely would have torn the child
Piecemeal among them, had they known; for each
But sought to rule for his own self and hand,
And many hated Uther for the sake
Of Gorloïs.   Wherefore Merlin took the child,   220
And gave him to Sir Anton, an old knight
And ancient friend of Uther, and his wife
Nursed the young prince, and reared him with her own;
And no man knew.   And ever since the lords
Have foughten like wild beasts among themselves,   225
So that the realm has gone to wrack : but now,
This year, when Merlin (for his hour had come)
Brought Arthur forth, and set him in the hall,
Proclaiming, "Here is Uther's heir, your king,"
A hundred voices cried, "Away with him!   230
No king of ours! a son of Gorloïs he;
Or else the child of Anton, and no king,
Or else baseborn."   Yet Merlin thro' his craft,
And while the people clamor'd for a king,
Had Arthur crown'd; but after, the great lords   235
Banded, and so brake out in open war.'

    Then while the King debated with himself
If Arthur were the child of shamefulness,
Or born the son of Gorloïs, after death,
Or Uther's son, and born before his time,   240
Or whether there were truth in anything

Said by these three, there came to Cameliard,
With Gawain and young Modred, her two sons,
Lot's wife, the Queen of Orkney, Bellicent;
Whom as he could, not as he would, the King   245
Made feast for, saying, as they sat at meat,

  'A doubtful throne is ice on summer seas.
Ye come from Arthur's court.   Victor his men
Report him!   Yea, but ye — think ye this king —
So many those that hate him, and so strong,   250
So few his knights, however brave they be —
Hath body enow to hold his foemen down?'

  'O King,' she cried, 'and I will tell thee: few,
Few, but all brave, all of one mind with him;
For I was near him when the savage yells   255
Of Uther's peerage died, and Arthur sat
Crown'd on the dais, and his warriors cried,
"Be thou the king, and we will work thy will
Who love thee."   Then the King in low deep tones,
And simple words of great authority,   260
Bound them by so strait vows to his own self,
That when they rose, knighted from kneeling, some
Were pale as at the passing of a ghost,
Some flush'd, and others dazed, as one who wakes
Half-blinded at the coming of a light.   265

  'But when he spake and cheer'd his Table Round
With large, divine, and comfortable words
Beyond my tongue to tell thee — I beheld
From eye to eye thro' all their Order flash
A momentary likeness of the King: 270
And ere it left their faces, thro' the cross

And those around it and the Crucified,
Down from the casement over Arthur, smote
Flame-color, vert and azure, in three rays,
One falling upon each of three fair queens,   275
Who stood in silence near his throne, the friends
Of Arthur, gazing on him, tall, with bright
Sweet faces, who will help him at his need.

' And there I saw mage Merlin, whose vast wit
And hundred winters are but as the hands   280
Of loyal vassals toiling for their liege.

' And near him stood the Lady of the Lake,
Who knows a subtler magic than his own —
Clothed in white samite, mystic, wonderful.
She gave the King his huge cross-hilted sword,   285
Whereby to drive the heathen out: a mist
Of incense curl'd about her, and her face
Wellnigh was hidden in the minster gloom;
But there was heard among the holy hymns
A voice as of the waters, for she dwells   290
Down in a deep; calm, whatsoever storms
May shake the world, and when the surface rolls,
Hath power to walk the waters like our Lord.

'There likewise I beheld Excalibur
Before him at his crowning borne, the sword   295
That rose from out the bosom of the lake,
And Arthur row'd across and took it — rich
With jewels, elfin Urim, on the hilt,
Bewildering heart and eye — the blade so bright
That men are blinded by it — on one side,   300
Graven in the oldest tongue of all this world,

" Take me," but turn the blade and ye shall see,
And written in the speech ye speak yourself,
"Cast me away!" And sad was Arthur's face
Taking it, but old Merlin counsell'd him,　　305
"Take thou and strike! the time to cast away
Is yet far-off." So this great brand the king
Took, and by this will beat his foemen down.'

　　Thereat Leodogran rejoiced, but thought
To sift his doubtings to the last, and ask'd,　　310
Fixing full eyes of question on her face,
'The swallow and the swift are near akin,
But thou art closer to this noble prince,
Being his own dear sister;' and she said,
'Daughter of Gorloïs and Ygerne am I;'　　315
'And therefore Arthur's sister?' ask'd the King.
She answered, 'These be secret things,' and sign'd
To those two sons to pass and let them be.
And Gawain went, and breaking into song
Sprang out, and follow'd by his flying hair　　320
Ran like a colt, and leapt at all he saw:
But Modred laid his ear beside the doors,
And there half-heard; the same that afterward
Struck for the throne, and striking found his doom.

　　And then the Queen made answer, ' What know I? 325
For dark my mother was in eyes and hair,
And dark in hair and eyes am I; and dark
Was Gorloïs, yea and dark was Uther too,
Wellnigh to blackness; but this King is fair
Beyond the race of Britons and of men.　　330
Moreover, always in my mind I hear
A cry from out the dawning of my life,

A mother weeping, and I hear her say,
"O that ye had some brother, pretty one,
To guard thee on the rough ways of the world." '   335

'Ay,' said the King, 'and hear ye such a cry?
But when did Arthur chance upon thee first?'

'O King,' she cried, 'and I will tell thee true:
He found me first when yet a little maid:
Beaten I had been for a little fault   340
Whereof I was not guilty; and out I ran
And flung myself down on a bank of heath,
And hated this fair world and all therein,
And wept, and wish'd that I were dead; and he —
I know not whether of himself he came,   34ⁿ
Or brought by Merlin, who, they say, can walk
Unseen at pleasure — he was at my side
And spake sweet words, and comforted my heart,
And dried my tears, being a child with me.
And many a time he came, and evermore   350
As I grew greater, grew with me; and sad
At times he seem'd, and sad with him was I,
Stern too at times, and then I loved him not,
But sweet again, and then I loved him well.
But now of late I see him less and less,   355
But those first days had golden hours for me,
For then I surely thought he would be king.

'But let me tell thee now another tale:
For Bleys, our Merlin's master, as they say,
Died but of late, and sent his cry to me,   360
To hear him speak before he left his life.
Shrunk like a fairy changeling lay the mage;
And when I enter'd told me that himself

And Merlin ever served about the King,
Uther, before he died; and on the night   365
When Uther in Tintagil past away
Moaning and wailing for an heir, the two
Left the still King, and passing forth to breathe,
Then from the castle gateway by the chasm
Descending thro' the dismal night — a night   370
In which the bounds of heaven and earth were lost—
Beheld, so high upon the dreary deeps
It seem'd in heaven, a ship, the shape thereof
A dragon wing'd, and all from stem to stern
Bright with a shining people on the decks,   375
And gone as soon as seen.   And then the two
Dropp'd to the cove, and watch'd the great sea fall,
Wave after wave, each mightier than the last,
Till last, a ninth one, gathering half the deep
And full of voices, slowly rose and plunged   380
Roaring, and all the wave was in a flame:
And down the wave and in the flame was borne
A naked babe, and rode to Merlin's feet,
Who stoop'd and caught the babe, and cried " The King!
Here is an heir for Uther!" and the fringe   385
Of that great breaker, sweeping up the strand,
Lash'd at the wizard as he spake the word,
And all at once all round him rose in fire,
So that the child and he were clothed in fire.
And presently thereafter follow'd calm,   390
Free sky and stars: " And this same child," he said,
" Is he who reigns; nor could I part in peace
Till this were told."   And saying this the seer
Went thro' the strait and dreadful pass of death,
Not ever to be question'd any more   395
Save on the further side; but when I met

Merlin, and ask'd him if these things were truth —
The shining dragon and the naked child
Descending in the glory of the seas —
He laugh'd as is his wont, and answer'd me   400
In riddling triplets of old time, and said: —

  '"Rain, rain, and sun! a rainbow in the sky'
A young man will be wiser by and by;
An old man's wit may wander ere he die.
    Rain, rain, and sun! a rainbow on the lea!   405
And truth is this to me, and that to thee;
And truth or clothed or naked let it be.
    Rain, sun, and rain! and the free blossom blows:
Sun, rain, and sun! and where is he who knows?
From the great deep to the great deep he goes."   410

  'So Merlin riddling anger'd me; but thou
Fear not to give this King thine only child,
Guinevere: so great bards of him will sing
Hereafter; and dark sayings from of old
Ranging and ringing thro' the minds of men,   415
And echoed by old folk beside their fires
For comfort after their wage-work is done,
Speak of the King; and Merlin in our time
Hath spoken also, not in jest, and sworn
Tho' men may wound him that he will not die   420
But pass, again to come; and then or now
Utterly smite the heathen underfoot,
Till these and all men hail him for their king'

  She spake and King Leodogran rejoiced,
But musing 'Shall I answer yea or nay?'   425
Doubted, and drowsed, nodded and slept, and saw,
Dreaming, a slope of land that ever grew,

Field after field, up to a height, the peak
Haze-hidden, and thereon a phantom king,
Now looming, and now lost; and on the slope   430
The sword rose, the hind fell, the herd was driven,
Fire glimpsed; and all the land from roof and rick,
In drifts of smoke before a rolling wind,
Stream'd to the peak, and mingled with the haze
And made it thicker; while the phantom king   435
Sent out at times a voice; and here or there
Stood one who pointed toward the voice, the rest
Slew on and burnt, crying, 'No king of ours,
No son of Uther, and no king of ours;'
Till with a wink his dream was changed, the haze   440
Descended, and the solid earth became
As nothing, but the King stood out in heaven,
Crown'd.   And Leodogran awoke, and sent
Ulfius, and Brastias and Bedivere,
Back to the court of Arthur answering yea.   445

    Then Arthur charged his warrior whom he loved
And honor'd most, Sir Lancelot, to ride forth
And bring the Queen; — and watch'd him from the gates:
And Lancelot pass'd away among the flowers,
(For then was latter April) and return'd   450
Among the flowers, in May, with Guinevere.
To whom arrived, by Dubric the high saint,
Chief of the church in Britain, and before
The stateliest of her altar-shrines, the King
That morn was married, while in stainless white   455
The fair beginners of a nobler time,
And glorying in their vows and him, his knights
Stood round him, and rejoicing in his joy.
Far shone the fields of May thro' open door,

The sacred altar blossom'd white with May,   460
The Sun of May descended on their King,
They gazed on all earth's beauty in their Queen,
Roll'd incense, and there pass'd along the hymns
A voice as of the waters, while the two
Sware at the shrine of Christ a deathless love :   465
And Arthur said, ' Behold, thy doom is mine.
Let chance what will, I love thee to the death ! '
To whom the Queen replied with drooping eyes,
' King and my lord, I love thee to the death ! '
And holy Dubric spread his hands and spake,   470
' Reign ye, and live and love, and make the world
Other, and may thy Queen be one with thee,
And all this Order of thy Table Round
Fulfil the boundless purpose of their King : '

    So Dubric said ; but when they left the shrine   475
Great Lords from Rome before the portal stood,
In scornful stillness gazing as they pass'd ;
Then while they paced a city all on fire
With sun and cloth of gold, the trumpets blew,
And Arthur's knighthood sang before the King · —   480

    ' Blow trumpet, for the world is white with May ;
Blow trumpet, the long night hath roll'd away !
Blow thro' the living world — "Let the King reign."

    ' Shall Rome or Heathen rule in Arthur's realm ?
Flash brand and lance, fall battleaxe upon helm,   485
Fall battleaxe, and flash brand ! Let the King reign.

    ' Strike for the King and live ! his knights have heard
That God hath told the King a secret word.
Fall battleaxe, and flash brand ! Let the King reign.

KING ARTHUR

'Blow trumpet! he will lift us from the dust.   490
Blow trumpet! live the strength and die the lust!
Clang battleaxe, and clash brand!   Let the King reign.

'Strike for the King and die! and if thou diest,
The King is King, and ever wills the highest.
Clang battleaxe, and clash brand!   Let the King reign.   495

'Blow, for our Sun is mighty in his May!
Blow, for our Sun is mightier day by day!
Clang battleaxe, and clash brand!   Let the King reign.

'The King will follow Christ, and we the King
In whom high God hath breathed a secret thing.   500
Fall battleaxe, and flash brand!   Let the King reign.'

So sang the knighthood, moving to their hall.
There at the banquet those great Lords from Rome,
The slowly-fading mistress of the world,
Strode in, and claim'd their tribute as of yore   505
But Arthur spake, 'Behold, for these have sworn
To wage my wars, and worship me their King;
The old order changeth, yielding place to new;
And we that fight for our fair father Christ.
Seeing that ye be grown too weak and old   510
To drive the heathen from your Roman wall,
No tribute will we pay ·' so those great Lords
Drew back in wrath, and Arthur strove with Rome.

And Arthur and his knighthood for a space
Were all one will, and thro' that strength the King   515
Drew in the petty princedoms under him,
Fought, and in twelve great battles overcame
The heathen hordes, and made a realm and reign'd.

GARETH AND LYNETTE.

THE last tall son of Lot and Bellicent,
And tallest, Gareth, in a showerful spring
Stared at the spate.   A slender-shafted Pine
Lost footing, fell, and so was whirl'd away.
'How he went down,' said Gareth, 'as a false knight   5
Or evil king before my lance, if lance
Were mine to use — O senseless cataract,
Bearing all down in thy precipitancy —
And yet thou art but swollen with cold snows
And mine is living blood: thou dost His will,   10
The Maker's, and not knowest, and I that know,
Have strength and wit, in my good mother's hall
Linger with vacillating obedience,
Prison'd, and kept and coax'd and whistled to —
Since the good mother holds me still a child!   15
Good mother is bad mother unto me !
A worse were better; yet no worse would I;
Heaven yield her for it, but in me put force
To weary her ears with one continuous prayer,
Until she let me fly discaged to sweep   20
In ever-highering eagle-circles up
To the great Sun of Glory, and thence swoop
Down upon all things base, and dash them dead,
A knight of Arthur, working out his will,
To cleanse the world.   Why, Gawain, when he came   25
With Modred hither in the summertime,
Ask'd me to tilt with him, the proven knight.
Modred for want of worthier was the judge.
Then I so shook him in the saddle, he said,
"Thou hast half prevail'd against me," said so — he —   30

Tho' Modred biting his thin lips was mute,
For he is alway sullen: what care I?'

And Gareth went, and hovering round her chair
Ask'd, 'Mother, tho' ye count me still the child,
Sweet mother, do ye love the child?'   She laugh'd,   35
'Thou art but a wild-goose to question it.'
'Then, mother, an ye love the child,' he said,
'Being a goose and rather tame than wild,
Hear the child's story.'   'Yea, my well-beloved,
An 'twere but of the goose and golden eggs.'   40

And Gareth answer'd her with kindling eyes,
'Nay, nay, good mother, but this egg of mine
Was finer gold than any goose can lay;
For this an Eagle, a royal Eagle, laid
Almost beyond eye-reach, on such a palm   45
As glitters gilded in thy Book of Hours.
And there was ever haunting round the palm
A lusty youth, but poor, who often saw
The splendor sparkling from aloft, and thought
"An I could climb and lay my hand upon it,   50
Then were I wealthier than a leash of kings."
But ever when he reach'd a hand to climb,
One, that had loved him from his childhood, caught
And stay'd him, "Climb not lest thou break thy neck,
I charge thee by my love," and so the boy,   55
Sweet mother, neither clomb nor brake his neck,
But brake his very heart in pining for it,
And pass'd away.'

                    To whom the mother said,
'True love, sweet son, had risk'd himself and climb'd,
And handed down the golden treasure to him.'   60

And Gareth answer'd her with kindling eyes,
'Gold? said I.gold?—ay then, why he, or she,
Or whosoe'er it was, or half the world
Had ventured—*had* the thing I spake of been
Mere gold—but this was all of that true steel,   65
Whereof they forged the brand Excalibur,
And lightnings play'd about it in the storm,
And all the little fowl were flurried at it,
And there were cries and clashings in the nest,
That sent him from his senses : let me go.'   70

Then Bellicent bemoan'd herself and said,
'Hast thou no pity upon my loneliness?
Lo, where thy father Lot beside the hearth
Lies like a log, and all but smoulder'd out!
For ever since when traitor to the King   75
He fought against him in the Barons' war,
And Arthur gave him back his territory,
His age hath slowly droop'd, and now lies there
A yet-warm corpse, and yet unburiable,
No more; nor sees, nor hears, nor speaks, nor knows   80
And both thy brethren are in Arthur's hall,
Albeit neither loved with that full love
I feel for thee, nor worthy such a love:
Stay therefore thou; red berries charm the bird,
And thee, mine innocent, the jousts, the wars,   85
Who never knewest finger-ache, nor pang
Of wrench'd or broken limb—and often chance
In those brain-stunning shocks, and tourney-falls,
Frights to my heart; but stay : follow the deer
By these tall firs and our fast falling burns;   90
So make thy manhood mightier day by day;
Sweet is the chase: and I will seek thee out

Some comfortable bride and fair, to grace
Thy climbing life, and cherish my prone year,
Till falling into Lot's forgetfulness   95
I know not thee, myself, nor anything.
Stay, my best son! ye are yet more boy than man.'

Then Gareth, 'An ye hold me yet for child,
Hear yet once more the story of the child.
For, mother, there was once a King, like ours.   100
The prince his heir, when tall and marriageable,
Ask'd for a bride; and thereupon the King
Set two before him. One was fair, strong, arm'd —
But to be won by force — and many men
Desired her; one, good lack, no man desired.   105
And these were the conditions of the King:
That save he won the first by force, he needs
Must wed that other, whom no man desired,
A red-faced bride who knew herself so vile,
That evermore she long'd to hide herself,   110
Nor fronted man or woman, eye to eye —
Yea — some she cleaved to, but they died of her.
And one — they call'd her Fame; and one, — O Mother,
How can ye keep me tether'd to you — Shame!
Man am I grown, a man's work must I do.   115
Follow the deer? follow the Christ, the King,
Live pure, speak true, right wrong, follow the King —
Else, wherefore born?'

                              To whom the mother said,
'Sweet son, for there be many who deem him not,
Or will not deem him, wholly proven King —   120
Albeit in mine own heart I knew him King,
When I was frequent with him in my youth,

And heard him kingly speak, and doubted him
No more than he, himself, but felt him mine,
Of closest kin to me; yet — wilt thou leave   125
Thine easeful biding here, and risk thine all,
Life, limbs, for one that is not proven King?
Stay, till the cloud that settles round his birth
Hath lifted but a little.   Stay, sweet son.'

    And Gareth answer'd quickly, 'Not an hour,   130
So that ye yield me — I will walk thro' fire,
Mother, to gain it · — your full leave to go.
Not proven, who swept the dust of ruin'd Rome
From off the threshold of the realm, and crush'd
The Idolaters, and made the people free?   135
Who should be King save him who makes us free?'

    So when the Queen, who long had sought in vain
To break him from the intent to which he grew,
Found her son's will unwaveringly one,
She answer'd craftily, 'Will ye walk thro' fire?   140
Who walks thro' fire will hardly heed the smoke.
Ay, go then, an ye must: only one proof,
Before thou ask the King to make thee knight,
Of thine obedience and thy love to me,
Thy mother, — I demand.'

                And Gareth cried,   145
'A hard one, or a hundred, so I go.
Nay — quick! the proof to prove me to the quick!'

    But slowly spake the mother looking at him,
'Prince, thou shalt go disguised to Arthur's hall,
And hire thyself to serve for meats and drinks   150

Among the scullions and the kitchen-knaves,
And those that hand the dish across the bar.
Nor shalt thou tell thy name to any one.
And thou shalt serve a twelvemonth and a day.'

For so the Queen believed that when her son   155
Beheld his only way to glory lead
Low down thro' villain kitchen-vassalage,
Her own true Gareth was too princely-proud
To pass thereby; so should he rest with her,
Closed in her castle from the sound of arms.   160

Silent awhile was Gareth, then replied,
'The thrall in person may be free in soul,
And I shall see the jousts. Thy son am I,
And since thou art my mother, must obey.
I therefore yield me freely to thy will;   165
For hence will I, disguised, and hire myself
To serve with scullions and with kitchen-knaves;
Nor tell my name to any — no, not the King.'

Gareth awhile linger'd. The mother's eye
Full of the wistful fear that he would go,   170
And turning toward him wheresoe'er he turn'd,
Perplext his outward purpose, till an hour,
When waken'd by the wind which with full voice
Swept bellowing thro' the darkness on to dawn,
He rose, and out of slumber calling two   175
That still had tended on him from his birth,
Before the wakeful mother heard him, went.

The three were clad like tillers of the soil.
Southward they set their faces. The birds made

Melody on branch, and melody in mid-air.   180
The damp hill-slopes were quicken'd into green.
And the live green had kindled into flowers,
For it was past the time of Easterday.

So, when their feet were planted on the plain
That broaden'd toward the base of Camelot,   185
Far off they saw the silver-misty morn
Rolling her smoke about the royal mount,
That rose between the forest and the field.
At times the summit of the high city flash'd;
At times the spires and turrets half-way down   190
Prick'd thro' the mist; at times the great gate shone
Only, that open'd on the field below:
Anon, the whole fair city had disappear'd.

Then those who went with Gareth were amazed,
One crying, 'Let us go no further, lord.   195
Here is a city of Enchanters, built
By fairy Kings.' The second echo'd him,
'Lord, we have heard from our wise man at home
To Northward, that this King is not the King,
But only changeling out of Fairyland,   200
Who drave the heathen hence by sorcery
And Merlin's glamour.' Then the first again,
'Lord, there is no such city anywhere,
But all a vision.'

        Gareth answer'd them
With laughter, swearing he had glamour enow   205
In his own blood, his princedom, youth and hopes,
To plunge old Merlin in the Arabian sea;
So push'd them all unwilling toward the gate.

And there was no gate like it under heaven,
For barefoot on the keystone, which was lined   210
And rippled like an ever-fleeting wave,
The Lady of the Lake stood: all her dress
Wept from her sides as water flowing away;
But like the cross her great and goodly arms
Stretch'd under all the cornice and upheld: 215
And drops of water fell from either hand;
And down from one a sword was hung, from one
A censer, either worn with wind and storm;
And o'er her breast floated the sacred fish;
And in the space to left of her, and right,   220
Were Arthur's wars in weird devices done,
New things and old co-twisted, as if Time
Were nothing, so inverately, that men
Were giddy gazing there; and over all
High on the top were those three Queens, the friends   225
Of Arthur, who should help him at his need.

  Then those with Gareth for so long a space
Stared at the figures, that at last it seem'd
The dragon-boughts and elvish emblemings
Began to move, seethe, twine and curl: they called   230
To Gareth, 'Lord, the gateway is alive.'

  And Gareth likewise on them fix'd his eyes
So long. that even to him they seem'd to move.
Out of the city a blast of music peal'd.
Back from the gate started the three, to whom   235
From out thereunder came an ancient man,
Long-bearded, saying, 'Who be ye, my sons?'

  Then Gareth, 'We be tillers of the soil,
Who leaving share in furrow come to see

The glories of our King: but these, my men,   240
(Your city moved so weirdly in the mist)
Doubt if the King be King at all, or come
From Fairyland; and whether this be built
By magic, and by fairy Kings and Queens;
Or whether there be any city at all,   245
Or all a vision: and this music now
Hath scared them both, but tell thou these the truth.'

Then that old Seer made answer playing on him,
And saying, 'Son, I have seen the good ship sail
Keel upward and mast downward in the heavens,   250
And solid turrets topsy-turvy in air:
And here is truth; but an it please thee not,
Take thou the truth as thou hast told it me.
For truly as thou sayest, a Fairy King
And Fairy Queens have built the city, son;   255
They came from out a sacred mountain-cleft
Toward the sunrise, each with harp in hand,
And built it to the music of their harps.
And as thou sayest, it is enchanted, son,
For there is nothing in it as it seems   260
Saving the King; tho' some there be that hold
The King a shadow, and the city real:
Yet take thou heed of him, for, so thou pass
Beneath this archway, then wilt thou become
A thrall to his enchantments, for the King   265
Will bind thee by such vows, as is a shame
A man should not be bound by, yet the which
No man can keep; but, so thou dread to swear,
Pass not beneath this gateway, but abide
Without, among the cattle of the field.   270
For an ye heard a music, like enow

They are building still, seeing the city is built
To music, therefore never built at all,
And therefore built forever.'

        Gareth spake
Anger'd, 'Old Master, reverence thine own beard   275
That looks as white as utter truth, and seems
Wellnigh as long as thou art statured tall!
Why mockest thou the stranger that hath been
To thee fair-spoken?'

        But the Seer replied,
'Know ye not then the Riddling of the Bards?   280
"Confusion, and elusion, and relation,
Elusion, and occasion, and evasion?"
I mock thee not, but as thou mockest me,
And all that see thee, for thou art not who
Thou seemest, but I know thee who thou art.   285
And now thou goest up to mock the King,
Who cannot brook the snadow of any lie.'

    Unmockingly the mocker ending here,
Turn'd to the right, and pass'd along the plain;
Whom Gareth looking after said, 'My men,   290
Our one white lie sits like . little ghost
Here on the threshold of our enterprise.
Let love be blamed for it, not she, nor I:
Well, we will make amends.'

        With all good cheer
He spake and laugh'd, then enter'd with his twain   294
Camelot, a city of shadowy palaces
And stately, rich in emblem and the work
Of ancient kings who did their days in stone,

Which Merlin's hand, the Mage at Arthur's court,
Knowing all arts, had touch'd, and everywhere   300
At Arthur's ordinance, tipp'd with lessening peak
And pinnacle, and had made it spire to heaven.
And ever and anon a knight would pass
Outward, or inward to the hall: his arms
Clash'd; and the sound was good to Gareth's ear.   305
And out of bower and casement shyly glanced
Eyes of pure women, wholesome stars of love.
And all about a healthful people stepp'd
As in the presence of a gracious king.

   Then into hall Gareth ascending heard   310
A voice, the voice of Arthur, and beheld
Far over heads in that long-vaulted hall
The splendor of the presence of the King
Throned, and delivering doom — and look'd no more —
But felt his young heart hammering in his ears,   315
And thought, 'For this half-shadow of a lie
The truthful King will doom me when I speak.'
Yet pressing on, tho' all in fear to find
Sir Gawain or Sir Modred, saw nor one
Nor other, but in all the listening eyes   320
Of those tall knights, that ranged about the throne,
Clear honor shining like the dewy star
Of dawn, and faith in their great King, with pure
Affection, and the light of victory,
And glory gain'd, and evermore to gain.   325

   Then came a widow crying to the King,
'A boon, Sir King! Thy father, Uther, reft
From my dead lord a field with violence:
For howsoe'er at first he proffer'd gold,

Yet, for the field was pleasant in our eyes,   330
We yielded not; and then he reft us of it
Perforce, and left us neither gold nor field.'

    Said Arthur, 'Whether would ye? gold or field?'
To whom the woman weeping, 'Nay, my lord,
The field was pleasant in my husband's eye.'   335

    And Arthur, 'Have thy pleasant field again,
And thrice the gold for Uther's use thereof,
According to the years.   No boon is here,
But justice, so thy say be proven true.
Accursed, who from the wrongs his father did   340
Would shape himself a right!'

                   And while she past
Came yet another widow crying to him,
'A boon, Sir King!   Thine enemy, King, am I.
With thine own hand thou slewest my dear lord,
A knight of Uther in the Barons' war,   345
When Lot and many another rose and fought
Against thee, saying thou wert basely born,
I held with these, and loathe to ask thee aught.
Yet lo! my husband's brother had my son
Thrall'd in his castle, and hath starved him dead;   350
And standeth seized of that inheritance
Which thou that slewest the sire hast left the son.
So tho' I scarce can ask it thee for hate,
Grant me some knight to do the battle for me,
Kill the foul thief, and wreak me for my son.'   355

    Then strode a good knight forward, crying to him,
'A boon, Sir King! I am her kinsman, I.
Give me to right her wrong, and slay the man.'

Then came Sir Kay, the seneschal, and cried,
'A boon, Sir King! even that thou grant her none,   **360**
This railer, that hath mock'd thee in full hall —
None; or the wholesome boon of gyve and gag.'

But Arthur, 'We sit King, to help the wrong'd
Thro' all our realm. The woman loves her lord.
Peace to thee, woman, with thy loves and hates!   **365**
The kings of old had doom'd thee to the flames,
Aurelius Emrys would have scourged thee dead,
And Uther slit thy tongue: but get thee hence —
Lest that rough humor of the kings of old
Return upon me! Thou that art her kin,   **370**
Go likewise; lay him low and slay him not,
But bring him here, that I may judge the right,
According to the justice of the King:
Then, be he guilty, by that deathless King
Who lived and died for men, the man shall die.'   **375**

Then came in hall the messenger of Mark,
A name of evil savor in the land,
The Cornish king. In either hand he bore
What dazzled all, and shone far-off as shines
A field of charlock in the sudden sun   **380**
Between two showers, a cloth of palest gold,
Which down he laid before the throne, and knelt,
Delivering, that his lord, the vassal king,
Was even upon his way to Camelot;
For having heard that Arthur of his grace   **385**
Had made his goodly cousin, Tristram, knight,
And, for himself was of the greater state,
Being a king, he trusted his liege-lord
Would yield him this large honor all the more;

So pray'd him well to accept this cloth of gold,   390
In token of true heart and fealty.

   Then Arthur cried to rend the cloth, to rend
In pieces, and so cast it on the hearth.
An oak-tree smoulder'd there. 'The goodly knight!
What! shall the shield of Mark stand among these?'   395
For, midway down the side of that long hall
A stately pile, — whereof along the front,
Some blazon'd, some but carven, and some blank,
There ran a treble range of stony shields, —
Rose, and high-arching overbrow'd the hearth.   400
And under every shield a knight was named:
For this was Arthur's custom in his hall;
When some good knight had done one noble deed,
His arms were carven only; but if twain
His arms were blazon'd also; but if none   405
The shield was blank and bare without a sign
Saving the name beneath; and Gareth saw
The shield of Gawain blazon'd rich and bright,
And Modred's blank as death; and Arthur cried
To rend the cloth and cast it on the hearth.   410

   'More like are we to reave him of his crown
Than make him knight because men call him king,
The kings we found, ye know we stay'd their hands
From war among themselves, but left them kings;
Of whom were any bounteous, merciful,   415
Truth-speaking, brave, good livers, them we enroll'd
Among us, and they sit within our hall.
But Mark hath tarnish'd the great name of king,
As Mark would sully the low state of churl:
And, seeing he hath sent us cloth of gold,   420

Return, and meet, and hold him from our eyes,
Lest we should lap him up in cloth of lead,
Silenced forever — craven — a man of plots,
Craft, poisonous counsels, wayside ambushings —
No fault of thine: let Kay the seneschal   425
Look to thy wants, and send thee satisfied —
Accursed, who strikes nor lets the hand be seen!'

And many another suppliant crying came
With noise of ravage wrought by beast and man,
And evermore a knight would ride away.   430

Last, Gareth leaning both hands heavily
Down on the shoulders of the twain, his men,
Approach'd between them toward the King, and ask'd,
'A boon, Sir King (his voice was all ashamed),
For see ye not how weak and hungerworn   435
I seem — leaning on these? grant me to serve
For meat and drink among thy kitchen-knaves
A twelvemonth and a day, nor seek my name.
Hereafter I will fight.'
                    To him the King,
'A goodly youth and worth a goodlier boon!   440
But so thou wilt no goodlier, then must Kay,
The master of the meats and drinks, be thine.'

He rose and past; then Kay, a man of mien
Wan-sallow as the plant that feels itself
Root-bitten by white lichen,
                         'Lo ye now!   445
This fellow hath broken from some Abbey, where,
God wot, he had not beef and brewis enow,
However that might chance! but an he work,
Like any pigeon will I cram his crop,
And sleeker shall he shine than any hog.'   450

Then Lancelot standing near, 'Sir Seneschal,
Sleuth-hound thou knowest, and gray, and all the hounds;
A horse thou knowest, a man thou dost not know:
Broad brows and fair, a fluent hair and fine,
High nose, a nostril large and fine, and hands   455
Large, fair and fine! — Some young lad's mystery —
But, or from sheepcot or king's hall, the boy
Is noble-natured.   Treat him with all grace,
Lest he should come to shame thy judging of him.'

Then Kay, 'What murmurest thou of mystery?   460
Think ye this fellow will poison the King's dish?
Nay, for he spake too fool-like: mystery!
Tut, an the lad were noble, he had ask'd
For horse and armor: fair and fine, forsooth!
Sir Fine-face, Sir Fair-hands? but see thou to it   465
That thine own fineness, Lancelot, some fine day
Undo thee not — and leave my man to me.'

So Gareth all for glory underwent
The sooty yoke of kitchen-vassalage;
Ate with young lads his portion by the door,   470
And couch'd at night with grimy kitchen-knaves.
And Lancelot ever spake him pleasantly,
But Kay the seneschal who loved him not
Would hustle and harry him, and labor him
Beyond his comrade of the hearth, and set   475
To turn the broach, draw water, or hew wood,
Or grosser tasks; and Gareth bow'd himself
With all obedience to the King, and wrought
All kind of service with a noble ease
That graced the lowliest act in doing it.   480
And when the thralls had talk among themselves,

And one would praise the love that link'd the King
And Lancelot — how the King had saved his life
In battle twice, and Lancelot once the King's —
For Lancelot was the first in Tournament,   485
But Arthur mightiest on the battle-field —
Gareth was glad.   Or if some other told,
How once the wandering forester at dawn,
Far over the blue tarns and hazy seas,
On Caer-Eryri's highest found the King,   490
A naked babe, of whom the Prophet spake,
'He passes to the Isle Avilion,
He passes and is heal'd and cannot die' —
Gareth was glad.   But if their talk were foul,
Then would he whistle rapid as any lark,   495
Or carol some old roundelay, and so loud
That first they mock'd, but, after, reverenced him
Or Gareth telling some prodigious tale
Of knights, who sliced a red life-bubbling way
Thro' twenty folds of twisted dragon, held   500
All in a gap-mouth'd circle his good mates
Lying or sitting round him, idle hands,
Charm'd; till Sir Kay, the seneschal, would come
Blustering upon them, like a sudden wind
Among dead leaves, and drive them all apart.   505
Or when the thralls had sport among themselves,
So there were any trial of mastery,
He, by two yards in casting bar or stone
Was counted best; and if there chanced a joust,
So that Sir Kay nodded him leave to go,   510
Would hurry thither, and when he saw the knights
Clash like the coming and retiring wave,
And the spear spring, and good horse reel, the boy
Was half beyond himself for ecstasy.

So for a month he wrought among the thralls; 515
But in the weeks that follow'd, the good Queen,
Repentant of the word she made him swear,
And saddening in her childless castle, sent.
Between the in-crescent and de-crescent moon,
Arms for her son, and loosed him from his vow. 520

This, Gareth hearing from a squire of Lot
With whom he used to play at tourney once,
When both were children, and in lonely haunts
Would scratch a ragged oval on the sand,
And each at either dash from either end — 525
Shame never made girl redder than Gareth joy.
He laugh'd; he sprang. 'Out of the smoke, at once
I leap from Satan's foot to Peter's knee —
These news be mine, none other's — nay, the King's —
Descend into the city:' whereon he sought 530
The King alone, and found, and told him all.

'I have stagger'd thy strong Gawain in a tilt
For pastime; yea, he said it: joust can I.
Make me thy knight — in secret! let my name
Be hidden, and give me the first quest, I spring 535
Like flame from ashes.'

                        Here the King's calm eye
Fell on, and check'd and made him flush, and bow
Lowly, to kiss his hand, who answer'd him,
'Son, the good mother let me know thee here,
And sent her wish that I would yield thee thine. 540
Make thee my knight? my knights are sworn to vows
Of utter hardihood, utter gentleness,
And, loving, utter faithfulness in love,
And uttermost obedience to the King.'

Then Gareth, lightly springing from his knees,   545
'My King, for hardihood I can promise thee.
For uttermost obedience make demand
Of whom you gave me to, the Seneschal,
No mellow master of the meats and drinks!
And as for love, God wot, I love not yet,   550
But love I shall, God willing.'

                        And the King—
'Make thee my knight in secret? yea, but he,
Our noblest brother, and our truest man,
And one with me in all, he needs must know.'

'Let Lancelot know, my King, let Lancelot know,   555
Thy noblest and thy truest!'

                        And the King—
'But wherefore would ye men should wonder at you?
Nay, rather for the sake of me, their King,
And the deed's sake my knighthood do the deed,
Than to be noised of.'

                        Merrily Gareth ask'd,   560
'Have I not earn'd my cake in baking of it?
Let be my name until I make my name!
My deeds will speak; it is but for a day.'
So with a kindly hand on Gareth's arm
Smiled the great King, and half-unwillingly,   565
Loving his lusty youthhood, yielded to him.
Then, after summoning Lancelot privily,
'I have given him the first quest: he is not proven,
Look therefore when he calls for this in hall,
Thou get to horse and follow him far away.   570
Cover the lions on thy shield, and see
Far as thou mayest, he be nor ta'en nor slain.'

Then that same day there pass'd into the hall
A damsel of high lineage, and a brow
May-blossom, and a cheek of apple-blossom,   575
Hawk-eyes ; and lightly was her slender nose
Tip-tilted like the petal of a flower ;
She into hall pass'd with her page and cried,

'O King, for thou hast driven the foe without,
See to the foe within ! bridge, ford, beset   580
By bandits, every one that owns a tower
The Lord for half a league.   Why sit ye there ?
Rest would I not, Sir King, an I were king,
Till even the lonest hold were all as free
From cursed bloodshed, as thine altar-cloth   585
From that best blood it is a sin tc spill.'

'Comfort thyself,' said Arthur, 'I nor mine
Rest : so my knighthood keep the vows they swore,
The wastest moorland of our realm shall be
Safe, damsel, as the centre of this hall.   590
What is thy name ? thy need ? '

                          'My name ? ' she said —
'Lynette my name ; noble ; my need, a knight
To combat for my sister, Lyonors,
A lady of high lineage, of great lands,
And comely, yea, and comelier than myself.   595
She lives in Castle Perilous : a river
Runs in three loops about her living-place ;
And o'er it are three passings, and three knights
Defend the passings, brethren, and a fourth
And of that four the mightiest, holds her stay'd   600
In her own castle, and so besieges her
To break her will, and make her wed with him :

And but delays his purport till thou send
To do the battle with him, thy chief man
Sir Lancelot whom he trusts to overthrow,   605
Then wed, with glory: but she will not wed
Save whom she loveth, or a holy life.
Now therefore have I come for Lancelot.'

  Then Arthur mindful of Sir Gareth ask'd,
'Damsel, ye know this Order lives to crush   610
All wrongers of the Realm.   But say, these four,
Who be they?   What the fashion of the men?'

  'They be of foolish fashion, O Sir King,
The fashion of that old knight-errantry
Who ride abroad and do but what they will;   615
Courteous or bestial from the moment, such
As have nor law nor king, and three of these
Proud in their fantasy call themselves the Day,
Morning-Star, and Noon-Sun, and Evening-Star,
Being strong fools; and never a whit more wise   620
The fourth, who alway rideth arm'd in black,
A huge man-beast of boundless savagery.
He names himself the Night and oftener Death,
And wears a helmet mounted with a skull,
And bears a skeleton figured on his arms,   625
To show that who may slay or scape the three
Slain by himself shall enter endless night.
And all these four be fools, but mighty men,
And therefore am I come for Lancelot.'

  Hereat Sir Gareth call'd from where he rose,   630
A head with kindling eyes above the throng,
'A boon, Sir King—this quest!' then—for he mark'd

Kay near him groaning like a wounded bull —
'Yea, King, thou knowest thy kitchen-knave am I,
And mighty thro' thy meats and drinks am I,   635
And I can topple over a hundred such.
Thy promise, King,' and Arthur glancing at him,
Brought down a momentary brow. 'Rough, sudden,
And pardonable, worthy to be knight —
Go therefore,' and all hearers were amazed.   640

    But on the damsel's forehead shame, pride, wrath
Slew the May-white: she lifted either arm,
'Fie on thee, King!   I ask'd for thy chief knight,
And thou hast given me but a kitchen-knave.'
Then ere a man in hall could stay her, turn'd,   645
Fled down the lane of access to the King,
Took horse, descended the slope street, and past
The weird white gate, and paused without, beside
The field of tourney, murmuring 'kitchen-knave.'

    Now two great entries open'd from the hall,   650
At one end one, that gave upon a range
Of level pavement where the King would pace
At sunrise, gazing over plain and wood;
And down from this a lordly stairway sloped
Till lost in blowing trees and tops of towers;   655
And out by this main doorway pass'd the King.
But one was counter to the hearth, and rose
High that the highest-crested helm could ride
Therethro' nor graze: and by this entry fled
The damsel in her wrath, and on to this   660
Sir Gareth strode, and saw without the door
King Arthur's gift, the worth of half a town,
A warhorse of the best, and near it stood

The two that out of north had follow'd him:
This bare a maiden shield, a casque; that held   665
The horse, the spear, whereat Sir Gareth loosed
A cloak that dropp'd from collar-bone to heel,
A cloth of roughest web, and cast it down,
And from it like a fuel-smother'd fire,
That look'd half-dead, brake bright, and flash'd as those 670
Dull-coated things, that making slide apart
Their dusk wing-cases, all beneath there burns
A jewell'd harness, ere they pass and fly.
So Gareth ere he parted flash'd in arms.
Then as he donn'd the helm, and took the shield   675
And mounted horse and grasp'd a spear, of grain
Storm-strengthen'd on a windy site, and tipp'd
With trenchant steel, around him slowly press'd
The people, while from out of kitchen came
The thralls in throng, and seeing who had work'd   680
Lustier than any, and whom they could but love,
Mounted in arms, threw up their caps and cried,
' God bless the King, and all his fellowship! '
And on thro' lanes of shouting Gareth rode
Down the slope street, and pass'd without the gate.   685

   So Gareth pass'd with joy; but as the cur
Pluck'd from the cur he fights with, ere his cause
Be cool'd by fighting, follows, being named,
His owner, but remembers all, and growls
Remembering, so Sir Kay beside the door   690
Mutter'd in scorn of Gareth whom he used
To harry and hustle.
                        ' Bound upon a quest
With horse and arms — the King hath pass'd his time —
My scullion knave! Thralls, to your work again,

For an your fire be low ye kindle mine !   695
Will there be dawn in West and eve in East ?
Begone ! — my knave ! — belike and like enow
Some old head-blow not heeded in his youth
So shook his wits they wander in his prime —
Crazed !   How the villain lifted up his voice,   700
Nor shamed to bawl himself a kitchen-knave.
Tut : he was tame and meek enow with me,
Till peacock'd up with Lancelot's noticing.
Well — I will after my loud knave, and learn
Whether he know me for his master yet.   705
Out of the smoke he came, and so my lance
Hold, by God's grace, he shall into the mire —
Thence, if the King awaken from his craze,
Into the smoke again.'

      But Lancelot said,
' Kay, wherefore wilt thou go against the King,   710
For that did never he whereon ye rail,
But ever meekly served the King in thee ?
Abide : take counsel ; for this lad is great
And lusty, and knowing both of lance and sword.'
' Tut, tell not me,' said Kay, ' ye are overfine   715
To mar stout knaves with foolish courtesies : '
Then mounted, on thro' silent faces rode
Down the slope city, and out beyond the gate.

  But by the field of tourney lingering yet
Mutter'd the damsel, ' Wherefore did the King   720
Scorn me ? for, were Sir Lancelot lack'd, at least
He might have yielded to me one of those
Who tilt for lady's love and glory here,
Rather than — O sweet heaven !   O fie upon him —
His kitchen-knave.'

                         To whom Sir Gareth drew   725
(And there were none but few goodlier than he)
Shining in arms, 'Damsel, the quest is mine.
Lead, and I follow.'   She thereat, as one
That smells a foul-flesh'd agaric in the holt,
And deems it carrion of some woodland thing,   730
Or shrew, or weasel, nipp'd her slender nose
With petulant thumb and finger, shrilling,
             'Hence!
Avoid, thou smellest all of kitchen-grease.
And look who comes behind,' for there was Kay.
'Knowest thou not me? thy master? I am Kay.   735
We lack thee by the hearth.'

                             And Gareth to him,
'Master no more! too well I know thee, ay—
The most ungentle knight in Arthur's hall.'
'Have at thee then,' said Kay: they shock'd, and Kay
Fell shoulder-slipp'd, and Gareth cried again,   740
'Lead, and I follow,' and fast away she fled.

   But after sod and shingle ceased to fly
Behind her, and the heart of her good horse
Was nigh to burst with violence of the beat,
Perforce she stay'd, and overtaken spoke: 745

   'What doest thou, scullion, in my fellowship?
Deem'st thou that I accept thee aught the more
Or love thee better, that by some device
Full cowardly, or by mere unhappiness,
Thou hast overthrown and slain thy master—thou!— 750
Dish-washer and broach-turner, loon!—to me
Thou smellest all of kitchen as before.'

'Damsel,' Sir Gareth answer'd gently, ' say
Whate'er ye will, but whatsoe'er ye say,
I leave not till I finish this fair quest,   755
Or die therefor.'

       ' Ay, wilt thou finish it ?
Sweet lord, how like a noble knight he talks !
The listening rogue hath caught the manner of it.
But, knave, anon thou shalt be met with, knave,
And then by such a one that thou for all   760
The kitchen brewis that was ever supp'd
Shalt not once dare to look him in the face.'

'I shall assay,' said Gareth with a smile
That madden'd her, and away she flash'd again
Down the long avenues of a boundless wood,   765
And Gareth following was again beknaved.

'Sir Kitchen-knave, I have miss'd the only way
Where Arthur's men are set along the wood;
The wood is nigh as full of thieves as leaves :
If both be slain, I am rid of thee; but yet,   770
Sir Scullion, canst thou use that spit of thine ?
Fight, an thou canst : I have miss'd the only way.'

So till the dusk that follow'd evensong
Rode on the two, reviler and reviled ;
Then after one long slope was mounted, saw,   775
Bowl-shaped, thro' tops of many thousand pines
A gloomy-gladed hollow slowly sink
To westward — in the deeps whereof a mere,
Round as the red eye of an Eagle-owl,
Under the half-dead sunset glared; and shouts   780
Ascended, and there brake a servingman

Flying from out of the black wood, and crying,
'They have bound my lord to cast him in the mere.'
Then Gareth, 'Bound am I to right the wrong'd,
But straitlier bound am I to bide with thee.'   785
And when the damsel spake contemptuously,
'Lead, and I follow,' Gareth cried again
'Follow, I lead!' so down among the pines
He plunged; and there, blackshadow'd nigh the mere,
And mid-thigh-deep in bulrushes and reed,   790
Saw six tall men haling a seventh along,
A stone about his neck to drown him in it.
Three with good blows he quieted, but three
Fled thro' the pines; and Gareth loosed the stone
From off his neck, then in the mere beside   795
Tumbled it; oilily bubbled up the mere.
Last, Gareth loosed his bonds, and on free feet
Set him, a stalwart Baron, Arthur's friend.

　'Well that ye came, or else these caitiff rogues
Had wreak'd themselves on me; good cause is theirs   800
To hate me, for my wont hath ever been
To catch my thief, and then like vermin here
Drown him, and with a stone about his neck;
And under this wan water many of them
Lie rotting, but at night let go the stone,   805
And rise, and flickering in a grimly light
Dance on the mere.　Good now, ye have saved a life
Worth somewhat as the cleanser of this wood,
And fain would I reward thee worshipfully.
What guerdon will ye?'

　　　　　　　　Gareth sharply spake,   811
'None! for the deed's sake have I done the deed,

In uttermost obedience to the King.
But wilt thou yield this damsel harborage?'

Whereat the Baron saying, 'I well believe
You be of Arthur's Table,' a light laugh   815
Broke from Lynette, 'Ay, truly of a truth,
And in a sort, being Arthur's kitchen-knave!—
But deem not I accept thee aught the more,
Scullion, for running sharply with thy spit
Down on a rout of craven foresters.   820
A thresher with his flail had scattered them.
Nay — for thou smellest of the kitchen still.
But an this lord will yield us harborage,
Well.'

So she spake. A league beyond the wood,
All in a full-fair manor and a rich,   825
His towers where that day a feast had been
Held in high hall, and many a viand left,
And many a costly cate, received the three.
And there they placed a peacock in his pride
Before the damsel, and the Baron set   830
Gareth beside her, but at once she rose.

'Meseems, that here is much discourtesy,
Setting this knave, Lord Baron, at my side.
Hear me — this morn I stood in Arthur's hall,
And pray'd the King would grant me Lancelot   835
To fight the brotherhood of Day and Night —
The last a monster unsubduable
Of any save of him for whom I call'd —
Suddenly bawls this frontless kitchen-knave,
" The quest is mine; thy kitchen-knave am I,   840

And mighty thro' thy meats and drinks am I."
Then Arthur all at once gone mad replies,
" Go therefore," and so gives the quest to him —
Him — here — a villain fitter to stick swine
Than ride abroad redressing women's wrong,   845
Or sit beside a noble gentlewoman.'

    Then half-ashamed and part-amazed, the lord
Now look'd at one and now at other; left
The damsel by the peacock in his pride,
And, seating Gareth at another board,   850
Sat down beside him, ate and then began.

    ' Friend, whether thou be kitchen-knave, or not,
Or whether it be the maiden's fantasy,
And whether she be mad, or else the King,
Or both or neither, or thyself be mad,   855
I ask not: but thou strikest a strong stroke,
For strong thou art and goodly therewithal,
And saver of my life ; and therefore now,
For here be mighty men to joust with, weigh
Whether thou wilt not with thy damsel back   860
To crave again Sir Lancelot of the King.
Thy pardon ; I but speak for thine avail,
The saver of my life.'

                And Gareth said,
' Full pardon, but I follow up the quest,
Despite of Day and Night and Death and Hell.'   865

    So when, next morn, the lord whose life he saved
Had, some brief space, convey'd them on their way
And left them with God-speed, Sir Gareth spake,
' Lead, and I follow.' Haughtily she replied,

'I fly no more: I allow thee for an hour.   870
Lion and stoat have isled together, knave,
In time of flood.   Nay, furthermore, methinks
Some ruth is mine for thee.   Back, wilt thou, fool?
For hard by here is one will overthrow
And slay thee: then will I to court again,   875
And shame the King for only yielding me
My champion from the ashes of his hearth.'

    To whom Sir Gareth answer'd courteously,
'Say thou thy say, and I will do my deed.
Allow me for mine hour, and thou wilt find   880
My fortunes all as fair as hers who lay
Among the ashes and wedded the King's son.'

    Then to the shore of one of those long loops
Wherethro' the serpent river coil'd, they came.
Rough-thicketed were the banks and steep; the stream   885
Full, narrow; this a bridge of single arc
Took at a leap; and on the further side
Arose a silk pavilion, gay with gold
In streaks and rays, and all Lent-lily in hue,
Save that the dome was purple, and above,   890
Crimson, a slender banneret fluttering.
And therebefore the lawless warrior paced
Unarm'd and calling, 'Damsel, is this he,
The champion thou hast brought from Arthur's hall?
For whom we let thee pass.'   'Nay, nay,' she said,   895
'Sir Morning-Star.   The King in utter scorn
Of thee and thy much folly hath sent thee here
His kitchen-knave: and look thou to thyself.
See that he fall not on thee suddenly,
And slay thee unarm'd: he is not knight but knave.'   900

Then at his call, ' O daughters of the Dawn,
And servants of the Morning-Star, approach,
Arm me,' from out the silken curtain-folds
Bare-footed and bare-headed three fair girls
In gilt and rosy raiment came : their feet   905
In dewy grasses glisten'd ; and the hair
All over glanced with dewdrop or with gem
Like sparkles in the stone Avanturine.
These arm'd him in blue arms, and gave a shield
Blue also, and thereon the morning star.   910
And Gareth silent gazed upon the knight,
Who stood a moment, ere his horse was brought,
Glorying ; and in the stream beneath him, shone
Immingled with Heaven's azure waveringly,
The gay pavilion and the naked feet,   915
His arms, the rosy raiment, and the star.

Then she that watch'd him, ' Wherefore stare ye so ?
Thou shakest in thy fear : there yet is time :
Flee down the valley before he get to horse.
Who will cry shame ?   Thou art not knight but knave.' 920

Said Gareth, ' Damsel, whether knave or knight,
Far liefer had I fight a score of times
Than hear thee so missay me and revile.
Fair words were best for him who fights for thee ;
But truly foul are better, for they send   925
That strength of anger thro' mine arms, I know
That I shall overthrow him.'

                         And he that bore
The star, being mounted, cried from o'er the bridge,
' A kitchen-knave, and sent in scorn of me !
Such fight not I, but answer scorn with scorn,   930

For this were shame to do him further wrong
Than set him on his feet, and take his horse
And arms, and so return him to the King.
Come, therefore, leave thy lady lightly, knave.
Avoid: for it beseemeth not a knave   935
To ride with such a lady.'

       'Dog, thou liest.
I spring from loftier lineage than thine own.'
He spake; and all at fiery speed the two
Shock'd on the central bridge, and either spear
Bent but not brake, and either knight at once,   940
Hurl'd as a stone from cut of a catapult
Beyond his horse's crupper and the bridge,
Fell, as if dead; but quickly rose and drew,
And Gareth lash'd so fiercely with his brand
He drave his enemy backward down the bridge,   945
The damsel crying, 'Well-stricken, kitchen-knave!'
Till Gareth's shield was cloven; but one stroke
Laid him that clove it grovelling on the ground.

 Then cried the fall'n, 'Take not my life: I yield.'
And Gareth, 'So this damsel ask it of me   950
Good — I accord it easily as a grace.'
She reddening, 'Insolent scullion: I of thee?
I bound to thee for any favor ask'd!'
'Then shall he die.' And Gareth there unlaced
His helmet as to slay him, but she shriek'd,   955
'Be not so hardy, scullion, as to slay
One nobler than thyself.' 'Damsel, thy charge
Is an abounding pleasure to me. Knight,
Thy life is thine at her command. Arise
And quickly pass to Arthur's hall, and say   960
His kitchen-knave hath sent thee. See thou crave

His pardon for thy breaking of his laws.
Myself, when I return, will plead for thee.
Thy shield is mine — farewell; and, damsel,
Lead, and I follow.'

                    And fast away she fled.   965
Then when he came upon her, spake, 'Methought,
Knave, when I watch'd thee striking on the bridge
The savour of thy kitchen came upon me
A little faintlier: but the wind hath changed:
I scent it twenty-fold.'   And then she sang,   970
' " O morning star " (not that tall felon there
Whom thou by sorcery or unhappiness
Or some device, hast foully overthrown),
" O morning star that smilest in the blue,
O star, my morning dream hath proven true,   975
Smile sweetly, thou! my love hath smiled on me."

'But thou begone, take counsel, and away,
For hard by here is one that guards a ford —
The second brother in their fool's parable —
Will pay thee all thy wages, and to boot.   980
Care not for shame: thou art not knight but knave.'

    To whom Sir Gareth answer'd, laughingly,
'Parables?   Hear a parable of the knave.
When I was kitchen-knave among the rest,
Fierce was the hearth, and one of my co-mates   985
Own'd a rough dog, to whom he cast his coat,
" Guard it," and there was none to meddle with it.
And such a coat art thou, and thee the King
Gave me to guard, and such a dog am I,
To worry, and not to flee — and — knight or knave —   990
The knave that doth thee service as full knight

Is all as good, meseems, as any knight
Toward thy sister's freeing.'

> 'Ay, Sir Knave!
Ay, knave, because thou strikest as a knight,
Being but knave, I hate thee all the more.'   99§

'Fair damsel, you should worship me the more,
That, being but knave, I throw thine enemies.'

'Ay, ay,' she said, 'but thou shalt meet thy match.'

So when they touch'd the second river-loop,
Huge on a huge red horse and all in mail   1000
Burnish'd to blinding, shone the Noonday Sun
Beyond a raging shallow.   As if the flower,
That blows a globe of after arrowlets,
Ten thousand fold had grown, flash'd the fierce shield,
All sun; and Gareth's eyes had flying blots   1005
Before them when he turn'd from watching him.
He from beyond the roaring shallow roar'd,
'What doest thou, brother, in my marches here?'
And she athwart the shallow shrill'd again,
'Here is a kitchen-knave from Arthur's hall   1010
Hath overthrown thy brother, and hath his arms.'
'Ugh!' cried the Sun, and vizoring up a red
And cipher face of rounded foolishness,
Push'd horse across the foamings of the ford,
Whom Gareth met midstream: no room was there   1015
For lance or tourney-skill: four strokes they struck
With sword, and these were mighty; the new knight
Had fear he might be shamed; but as the Sun
Heaved up a ponderous arm to strike the fifth,
The hoof of his horse slipp'd in the stream, the stream 1020
Descended, and the Sun was wash'd away.

Then Gareth laid his lance athwart the ford;
So drew him home; but he that fought no more,
As being all bone-batter'd on the rock,
Yielded; and Gareth sent him to the King.   1025
'Myself when I return will plead for thee.'
'Lead, and I follow.'   Quietly she led.
'Hath not the good wind, damsel, changed again?'
'Nay, not a point: nor art thou victor here.
There lies a ridge of slate across the ford;   1030
His horse thereon stumbled — ay, for I saw it.

  '"O Sun" (not this strong fool whom thou, Sir Knave,
Hast overthrown thro' mere unhappiness),
"O Sun, that wakenest all to bliss or pain,
O moon, that layest all to sleep again,   1035
Shine sweetly: twice my love hath smiled on me."

  'What knowest thou of lovesong or of love?
Nay, nay, God wot, so thou wert nobly born,
Thou hast a pleasant presence.   Yea, perchance, —

  '"O dewy flowers that open to the sun,   1040
O dewy flowers that close when day is done,
Blow sweetly: twice my love hath smiled on me."

  'What knowest thou of flowers, except, belike,
To garnish meats with? hath not our good King
Who lent me thee, the flower of kitchendom,   1045
A foolish love for flowers? what stick ye round
The pasty? wherewithal deck the boar's head?
Flowers? nay, the boar hath rosemaries and bay.

  '"O birds that warble to the morning sky,
O birds that warble as the day goes by,   1050
Sing sweetly: twice my love hath smiled on me."

'What knowest thou of birds, lark, mavis, merle,
Linnet? what dream ye when they utter forth
May-music growing with the growing light,
Their sweet sun-worship? these be for the snare   1055
(So runs thy fancy), these be for the spit,
Larding and basting. See thou have not now
Larded thy last, except thou turn and fly
There stands the third fool of their allegory.'

For there beyond a bridge of treble bow,   1060
All in a rose-red from the west, and all
Naked it seem'd, and glowing in the broad
Deep-dimpled current underneath, the knight,
That named himself the Star of Evening, stood.

And Gareth, 'Wherefore waits the madman there   1065
Naked in open dayshine?' 'Nay,' she cried,
'Not naked, only wrapp'd in harden'd skins
That fit him like his own; and so ye cleave
His armor off him, these will turn the blade.'

Then the third brother shouted o'er the bridge,   1070
'O brother-star, why shine ye here so low?
Thy ward is higher up: but have ye slain
The damsel's champion?' and the damsel cried,

'No star of thine, but shot from Arthur's heaven
With all disaster unto thine and thee!   1075
For both thy younger brethren have gone down
Before this youth; and so wilt thou, Sir Star;
Art thou not old?'

                    'Old, damsel, old and hard,
Old, with the might and breath of twenty boys.'
Said Gareth, 'Old, and over-bold in brag!   1080

But that same strength which threw the Morning Star
Can throw the Evening.'
                          Then that other blew
A hard and deadly note upon the horn.
'Approach and arm me!'   With slow steps from out
An old storm-beaten, russet, many-stain'd   108|
Pavilion, forth a grizzled damsel came,
And arm'd him in old arms, and brought a helm
With but a drying evergreen for crest,
And gave a shield whereon the Star of Even
Half-tarnish'd and half-bright, his emblem, shone.   1090
But when it glitter'd o'er the saddle-bow,
They madly hurl'd together on the bridge;
And Gareth overthrew him, lighted, drew,
There met him drawn, and overthrew him again,
But up like fire he started: and as oft   1095
As Gareth brought him grovelling on his knees,
So many a time he vaulted up again;
Till Gareth panted hard, and his great heart,
Foredooming all his trouble was in vain,
Labor'd within him, for he seem'd as one   1100
That all in later, sadder age begins
To war against ill uses of a life,
But these from all his life arise, and cry,
'Thou hast made us lords, and canst not put us down!'
He half despairs; so Gareth seem'd to strike   1105
Vainly, the damsel clamoring all the while,
'Well done, knave-knight, well stricken, O good knight
          knave—
O knave, as noble as any of all the knights—
Shame me not, shame me not.   I have prophesied—
Strike, thou art worthy of the Table Round—   1110
His arms are old, he trusts the harden'd skin—

Strike — strike — the wind will never change again.'
And Gareth hearing ever stronglier smote,
And hew'd great pieces of his armor off him,
But lash'd in vain against the harden'd skin,   **1115**
And could not wholly bring him under, more
Than loud Southwesterns, rolling ridge on ridge,
The buoy that rides at sea, and dips and springs
Forever; till at length Sir Gareth's brand
Clash'd his, and brake it utterly to the hilt.   **1120**
I have thee now;' but forth that other sprang,
And, all unknightlike, writhed his wiry arms
Around him, till he felt, despite his mail,
Strangled, but straining even his uttermost
Cast, and so hurl'd him headlong o'er the bridge   **1125**
Down to the river, sink or swim, and cried,
Lead, and I follow.'

                              But the damsel said,
I lead no longer; ride thou at my side;
Thou art the kingliest of all kitchen-knaves.

 ' "O trefoil, sparkling on the rainy plain,   **1130**
O rainbow with three colors after rain,
Shine sweetly; thrice my love has smiled on me."

'Sir, — and, good faith, I fain had added — Knight,
But that I heard thee call thyself a knave, —
Shamed am I that I so rebuked, reviled,   **1135**
Missaid thee; noble I am; and thought the King
Scorn'd me and mine; and now thy pardon, friend,
For thou hast ever answer'd courteously,
And wholly bold thou art, and meek withal
As any of Arthur's best, but, being knave,   **1140**
Hast mazed my wit: I marvel what thou art.'

'Damsel,' he said, 'you be not all to blame,
Saving that you mistrusted our good King
Would handle scorn, or yield you, asking, one
Not fit to cope your quest.   You said your say;   1145
Mine answer was my deed.   Good sooth! I hold
He scarce is knight, yea but half-man, nor meet
To fight for gentle damsel, he, who lets
His heart be stirr'd with any foolish heat
At any gentle damsel's waywardness.   1150
Shamed? care not! thy foul sayings fought for me:
And seeing now thy words are fair, methinks
There rides no knight, not Lancelot, his great self,
Hath force to quell me.'
                              Nigh upon that hour
When the lone hern forgets his melancholy,   1155
Lets down his other leg, and stretching, dreams
Of goodly supper in the distant pool,
Then turn'd the noble damsel smiling at him,
And told him of a cavern hard at hand,
Where bread and baked meats and good red wine   1160
Of southland, which the Lady Lyonors
Had sent her coming champion, waited him.

    Anon they past a narrow comb wherein
Were slabs of rock with figures, knights on horse
Sculptured, and deckt in slowly-waning hues.   1165
'Sir Knave, my knight, a hermit once was here,
Whose holy hand hath fashion'd on the rock
The war of Time against the soul of man,
And yon four fools have suck'd their allegory
From these damp walls and taken but the form.   1170
Know ye not these?' and Gareth look'd and read—
In letters like to those the vexillary

Hath left crag-carven o'er the streaming Gelt —
'PHOSPHORUS,' then, 'MERIDIES'— 'HESPERUS' —
'Nox'—'MORS,' beneath five figures, armed men.   1175
Slab after slab, their faces forward all,
And running down the Soul, a Shape that fled
With broken wings, torn raiment and loose hair,
For help and shelter to the hermit's cave.
'Follow the faces, and we find it. Look,   1180
Who comes behind?'

            For one — delay'd at first
Thro' helping back the dislocated Kay
To Camelot, then by what thereafter chanced,
The damsel's headlong error thro' the wood —
Sir Lancelot, having swum the river-loops —   1185
His blue shield-lions cover'd — softly drew
Behind the twain, and when he saw the star
Gleam, on Sir Gareth's turning to him, cried,
'Stay, felon knight, I avenge me for my friend.'
And Gareth crying prick'd against the cry;   1190
But when they closed — in a moment — at one touch
Of that skill'd spear, the wonder of the world —
Went sliding down so easily, and fell,
That when he found the grass within his hands
He laugh'd; the laughter jarr'd upon Lynette: 1195
Harshly she ask'd him, 'Shamed and overthrown,
And tumbled back into the kitchen-knave,
Why laugh ye? that ye blew your boast in vain?'
'Nay, noble damsel, but that I, the son
Of old King Lot and good Queen Bellicent,   1200
And victor of the bridges and the ford,
And knight of Arthur, here lie thrown by whom
I know not, all thro' mere unhappiness —
Device and sorcery and unhappiness —

Out, sword; we are thrown!' And Lancelot answer'd,
        'Prince,   1205
O Gareth — thro' the mere unhappiness
Of one who came to help thee, not to harm,
Lancelot, and all as glad to find thee whole,
As on the day when Arthur knighted him.'

    Then Gareth, 'Thou — Lancelot! — thine the hand   1210
That threw me? An some chance to mar the boast
Thy brethren of thee make — which could not chance —
Had sent thee down before a lesser spear,
Shamed had I been, and sad — O Lancelot — thou!'

    Whereat the maiden, petulant, 'Lancelot,   1215
Why came ye not, when call'd? and wherefore now
Come ye, not call'd? I gloried in my knave,
Who being still rebuked, would answer still
Courteous as any knight — but now, if knight,
The marvel dies, and leaves me fool'd and trick'd   1220
And only wondering wherefore play'd upon:
And doubtful whether I and mine be scorn'd.
Where should be truth if not in Arthur's hall,
In Arthur's presence? Knight, knave, prince and fool,
I hate thee and forever.'

                            And Lancelot said,   1225
'Blessed be thou, Sir Gareth! knight art thou
To the King's best wish. O damsel, be you wise
To call him shamed, who is but overthrown?
Thrown have I been, nor once, but many a time.
Victor from vanquish'd issues at the last,   1230
And overthrower from being overthrown.
With sword we have not striven; and thy good horse
And thou are weary; yet not less I felt

Thy manhood thro' that wearied lance of thine.
Well hast thou done; for all the stream is freed,   1235
And thou hast wreak'd his justice on his foes,
And when reviled, hast answer'd graciously,
And makest merry when overthrown.   Prince, Knight,
Hail, Knight and Prince, and of our Table Round!'

    And then when turning to Lynette he told   1240
The tale of Gareth, petulantly she said,
'Ay well — ay well — for worse than being fool'd
Of others, is to fool one's self.   A cave,
Sir Lancelot, is hard by, with meats and drinks
And forage for the horse, and flint for fire.   1245
But all about it flies a honeysuckle.
Seek, till we find.'   And when they sought and found,
Sir Gareth drank and ate, and all his life
Pass'd into sleep; on whom the maiden gazed.
'Sound sleep be thine! sound cause to sleep hast thou.   1250
Wake lusty!   Seem I not as tender to him
As any mother?   Ay, but such a one
As all day long hath rated at her child,
And vex'd his day, but blesses him asleep —
Good lord, how sweetly smells the honeysuckle   1255
In the hush'd night, as if the world were one
Of utter peace, and love, and gentleness!
O Lancelot, Lancelot' — and she clapt her hands —
'Full merry am I to find my goodly knave
Is knight and noble.   See now, sworn have I,   1260
Else yon black felon had not let me pass,
To bring thee back to do the battle with him.
Thus an thou goest, he will fight thee first;
Who doubts thee victor? so will my knight-knave
Miss the full flower of this accomplishment.',   1265

Said Lancelot, 'Peradventure he, you name,
May know my shield.   Let Gareth, an he will,
Change his for mine, and take my charger, fresh,
Not to be spurr'd, loving the battle as well
As he that rides him.'   'Lancelot-like,' she said,   1270
'Courteous in this, Lord Lancelot, as in all.'

   And Gareth, wakening, fiercely clutch'd the shield;
'Ramp, ye lance-splintering lions, on whom all spears
Are rotten sticks! ye seem agape to roar!
Yea, ramp and roar at leaving of your lord!—   1275
Care not, good beasts, so well I care for you.
O noble Lancelot, from my hold on these
Streams virtue—fire—thro' one that will not shame
Even the shadow of Lancelot under shield.
Hence: let us go.'
                    Silent the silent field   1280
They traversed.   Arthur's harp tho' summer-wan,
In counter motion to the clouds, allured
The glance of Gareth dreaming on his liege.
A star shot: 'Lo,' said Gareth, 'the foe falls!'
An owl whoop'd: 'Hark the victor pealing there!'   1285
Suddenly she that rode upon his left
Clung to the shield that Lancelot lent him, crying,
'Yield, yield him this again; 'tis he must fight:
I curse the tongue that all thro' yesterday
Reviled thee, and hath wrought on Lancelot now   1290
To lend thee horse and shield: wonders ye have done;
Miracles ye cannot: here is glory enow
In having flung the three: I see thee maim'd,
Mangled: I swear thou canst not fling the fourth.'

   'And wherefore, damsel? tell me all ye know.   1295
You cannot scare me; nor rough face, or voice,

Brute bulk of limb, or boundless savagery
Appal me from the quest.'

           'Nay, Prince,' she cried,
'God wot, I never look'd upon the face,
Seeing he never rides abroad by day;
But watch'd him have I like a phantom pass   1300
Chilling the night: nor have I heard the voice.
Always he made his mouthpiece of a page
Who came and went, and still reported him
As closing in himself the strength of ten,   1305
And when his anger tare him, massacring
Man, woman, lad and girl — yea, the soft babe:
Some hold that he hath swallow'd infant flesh,
Monster! O Prince, I went for Lancelot first,
The quest is Lancelot's: give him back the shield.'   1310

   Said Gareth laughing, 'An he fight for this,
Belike he wins it as the better man:
Thus — and not else!'

          But Lancelot on him urged
All the devisings of their chivalry
When one might meet a mightier than himself;   1315
How best to manage horse, lance, sword, and shield,
And so fill up the gap where force might fail
With skill and fineness. Instant were his words.

   Then Gareth, 'Here be rules. I know but one —
To dash against mine enemy and to win.   1320
Yet have I watch'd thee victor in the joust,
And seen thy way.' 'Heaven help thee,' sigh'd Lynette.

   Then for a space, and under cloud that grew
To thunder-gloom palling all stars, they rode

In converse till she made her palfrey halt,   1325
Lifted an arm, and softly whisper'd, 'There.'
And all the three were silent seeing, pitch'd
Beside the Castle Perilous on flat field,
A huge pavilion like a mountain peak
Sunder the glooming crimson on the marge,   1330
Black, with black banner, and a long black horn
Beside it hanging; which Sir Gareth grasp'd,
And so, before the two could hinder him,
Sent all his heart and breath thro' all the horn.
Echoed the walls; a light twinkled; anon   1335
Came lights and lights, and once again he blew;
Whereon were hollow tramplings up and down
And muffled voices heard, and shadows past;
Till high above him, circled with her maids,
The Lady Lyonors at a window stood,   1340
Beautiful among lights, and waving to him
White hands, and courtesy; but when the Prince
Three times had blown — after long hush — at last —
The huge pavilion slowly yielded up,
Thro' those black foldings, that which housed therein.   1345
High on a nightblack horse, in nightblack arms,
With white breast-bone, and barren ribs of Death,
And crown'd with fleshless laughter — some ten steps —
In the half-light — thro' the dim dawn — advanced
The monster, and then paused, and spake no word.   1350

    But Gareth spake and all indignantly,
'Fool, for thou hast, men say, the strength of ten,
Canst thou not trust the limbs thy God hath given,
But must, to make the terror of thee more,
Trick thyself out in ghastly imageries   1355
Of that which Life hath done with, and the clod,

Less dull than thou, will hide with mantling flowers
As if for pity ?'   But he spake no word ;
Which set the horror higher: a maiden swoon'd ;
The Lady Lyonors wrung her hands and wept,   1360
As doom'd to be the bride of Night and Death ;
Sir Gareth's head prickled beneath his helm ;
And even Sir Lancelot thro' his warm blood felt
Ice strike ; and all that mark'd him were aghast.
At once Sir Lancelot's charger fiercely neigh'd   1365
And Death's dark war-horse bounded forward with him.
Then those that did not blink the terror, saw
That Death was cast to ground, and slowly rose.
But with one stroke Sir Gareth split the skull.
Half fell to right and half to left and lay.   1370
Then with a stronger buffet he clove the helm
As thoroughly as the skull ; and out from this
Issued the bright face of a blooming boy
Fresh as a flower new-born, and crying, 'Knight,
Slay me not: my three brethren bade me do it,   1375
To make a horror all about the house,
And stay the world from Lady Lyonors.
They never dream'd the passes would be pass'd.'
Answer'd Sir Gareth graciously to one
Not many a moon his younger, 'My fair child,   1380
What madness made thee challenge the chief knight
Of Arthur's hall ?'   'Fair Sir, they bade me do it.
They hate the King, and Lancelot, the King's friend,
They hoped to slay him somewhere on the stream,
They never dream'd the passes could be pass'd.'   1385

   Then sprang the happier day from underground ;
And Lady Lyonors and her house, with dance
And revel and song, made merry over Death,

As being after all their foolish fears
And horrors only proven a blooming boy.   1390
So large mirth lived and Gareth won the quest.

And he that told the tale in older times
Says that Sir Gareth wedded Lyonors,
But he that told it later, says Lynette.

LANCELOT AND ELAINE.

ELAINE the fair, Elaine the lovable,
Elaine, the lily maid of Astolat,
High in her chamber up a tower to the east
Guarded the sacred shield of Lancelot;
Which first she placed where morning's earliest ray   5
Might strike it, and awake her with the gleam;
Then fearing rust or soilure fashion'd for it
A case of silk, and braided thereupon
All the devices blazon'd on the shield
In their own tinct, and added, of her wit,   10
A border fantasy of branch and flower,
And yellow-throated nestling in the nest.
Nor rested thus content, but day by day,
Leaving her household and good father, climb'd
That eastern tower, and entering barr'd her door,   15
Stripp'd off the case, and read the naked shield,
Now guess'd a hidden meaning in his arms,
Now made a pretty history to herself
Of every dint a sword had beaten in it,
And every scratch a lance had made upon it,   20
Conjecturing when and where: this cut is fresh;
That ten years back: this dealt him at Caerlyle;
That at Caerleon; this at Camelot:
And ah God's mercy, what a stroke was there!
And here a thrust that might have kill'd, but God   25
Broke the strong lance, and roll'd his enemy down,
And saved him: so she lived in fantasy.

How came the lily maid by that good shield
Of Lancelot, she that knew not even his name?

He left it with her, when he rode to tilt   30
For the great diamond in the diamond jousts,
Which Arthur had ordain'd, and by that name
Had named them, since a diamond was the prize.

For Arthur, long before they crown'd him King,
Roving the trackless realms of Lyonnesse,   35
Had found a glen, gray boulder and black tarn.
A horror lived about the tarn, and clave
Like its own mists to all the mountain side:
For here two brothers, one a king, had met
And fought together; but their names were lost;   40
And each had slain his brother at a blow;
And down they fell and made the glen abhorr'd:
And there they lay till all their bones were bleach'd,
And lichen'd into color with the crags:
And he, that once was a king, had on a crown   45
Of diamonds, one in front, and four aside.
And Arthur came, and laboring up the pass,
All in a misty moonshine, unawares
Had trodden that crown'd skeleton, and the skull
Brake from the nape, and from the skull the crown   50
Roll'd into light, and turning on its rims
Fled like a glittering rivulet to the tarn:
And down the shingly scaur he plunged, and caught,
And set it on his head, and in his heart
Heard murmurs, 'Lo, thou likewise shalt be King.'   55

    Thereafter, when a King, he had the gems
Pluck'd from the crown, and show'd them to his knights,
Saying, 'These jewels, whereupon I chanced
Divinely, are the kingdom's, not the King's —
For public use; henceforward let there be,   60

ARTHUR DISCOVERS THE SKELETONS OF THE TWO BROTHERS.

Once every year, a joust for one of these:
For so by nine years' proof we need must learn
Which is our mightiest, and ourselves shall grow
In use of arms and manhood, till we drive
The heathen, who, some say, shall rule the land   **65**
Hereafter, which God hinder.'   Thus he spoke:
And eight years pass'd, eight jousts had been, and still
Had Lancelot won the diamond of the year,
With purpose to present them to the Queen,
When all were won; but meaning all at once   **70**
To snare her royal fancy with a boon
Worth half her realm, had never spoken word.

   Now for the central diamond and the last
And largest, Arthur, holding then his court
Hard on the river nigh the place which now   **75**
Is this world's hugest, let proclaim a joust
At Camelot, and when the time drew nigh
Spake (for she had been sick) to Guinevere,
'Are you so sick, my Queen, you cannot move
To these fair jousts?' 'Yea, lord,' she said, 'ye know it.' **80**
'Then will ye miss,' he answer'd, 'the great deeds
Of Lancelot, and his prowess in the lists,
A sight ye love to look on.'   And the Queen
Lifted her eyes, and they dwelt languidly
On Lancelot, where he stood beside the King.   **85**
He thinking that he read her meaning there,
'Stay with me, I am sick; my love is more
Than many diamonds,' yielded: and a heart
Love-loyal to the least wish of the Queen
(However much he yearn'd to make complete   **90**
The tale of diamonds for his destined boon)
Urged him to speak against the truth, and say,

'Sir King, mine ancient wound is hardly whole,
And lets me from the saddle;' and the King
Glanced first at him, then her, and went his way.   95
No sooner gone than suddenly she began:

'To blame, my lord Sir Lancelot, much to blame!
Why go ye not to these fair jousts? the knights
Are half of them our enemies, and the crowd
Will murmur, " Lo the shameless ones, who take   100
Their pastime now the trustful King is gone!"'
Then Lancelot, vex'd at having lied in vain:
'Are ye so wise? ye were not once so wise,
My Queen, that summer, when ye loved me first.
Then of the crowd ye took no more account   105
Than of the myriad cricket of the mead,
When its own voice clings to each blade of grass,
And every voice is nothing.   As to knights,
Them surely can I silence with all ease.
But now my loyal worship is allow'd   110
Of all men: many a bard, without offence,
Has link'd our names together in his lay,
Lancelot, the flower of bravery, Guinevere,
The pearl of beauty; and our knights at feast
Have pledged us in this union, while the King   115
Would listen smiling.   How then? is there more?
Has Arthur spoken aught? or would yourself,
Now weary of my service and devoir,
Henceforth be truer to your faultless lord?'

She broke into a little scornful laugh: 120
'Arthur, my lord, Arthur, the faultless King,
That passionate perfection, my good lord —
But who can gaze upon the Sun in heaven?

He never spake word of reproach to me,
He never had a glimpse of mine untruth, 125
He cares not for me: only here to-day
There gleam'd a vague suspicion in his eyes:
Some meddling rogue has tamper'd with him — else
Rapt in this fancy of his Table Round,
And swearing men to vows impossible, 130
To make them like himself: but, friend, to me
He is all fault who hath no fault at all:
For who loves me must have a touch of earth;
The low sun makes the color: I am yours,
Not Arthur's, as ye know, save by the bond. 135
And therefore hear my words: go to the jousts:
The tiny-trumpeting gnat can break our dream
When sweetest; and the vermin voices here
May buzz so loud — we scorn them, but they sting.'

  Then answer'd Lancelot, the chief of knights: 140
'And with what face, after my pretext made,
Shall I appear, O Queen, at Camelot, I
Before a King who honors his own word
As if it were his God's?'

                      'Yea,' said the Queen,
'A moral child without the craft to rule, 145
Else had he not lost me: but listen to me,
If I must find you wit: we hear it said
That men go down before your spear at a touch,
But knowing you are Lancelot; your great name,
This conquers: hide it therefore; go unknown: 150
Win! by this kiss you will; and our true King
Will then allow your pretext, O my knight,
As all for glory; for to speak him true,

Ye know right well, how meek soe'er he seem,
No keener hunter after glory breathes.   155
He loves it in his knights more than himself:
Then prove to him his work: win and return.'

    Then got Sir Lancelot suddenly to horse,
Wroth at himself.   Not willing to be known,
He left the barren-beaten thoroughfare   160
Chose the green path that show'd the rarer foot,
And there among the solitary downs,
Full often lost in fancy, lost his way;
Till as he traced a faintly-shadow'd track,
That all in loops and links among the dales   165
Ran to the Castle of Astolat, he saw
Fired from the west, far on a hill, the towers.
Thither he made, and blew the gateway horn.
Then came an old, dumb, myriad-wrinkled man,
Who let him into lodging and disarm'd.   170
And Lancelot marvell'd at the wordless man;
And issuing found the Lord of Astolat
With two strong sons, Sir Torre and Sir Lavaine,
Moving to meet him in the castle court;
And close behind them stept the lily maid   175
Elaine, his daughter: mother of the house
There was not: some light jest among them rose
With laughter dying down as the great knight
Approach'd them: then the Lord of Astolat:
'Whence comest thou, my guest, and by what name   180
Livest between the lips? for by thy state
And presence I might guess thee chief of those,
After the King, who eat in Arthur's halls.
Him have I seen: the rest, his Table Round,
Known as they are, to me they are unknown.'   185

Then answer'd Lancelot, the chief of knights :
'Known am I, and of Arthur's hall, and known,
What I by mere mischance have brought, my shield.
But since I go to joust as one unknown
At Camelot for the diamond, ask me not,   190
Hereafter ye shall know me — and the shield —
I pray you lend me one, if such you have,
Blank, or at least with some device not mine.'

Then said the Lord of Astolat, 'Here is Torre's :
Hurt in his first tilt was my son, Sir Torre.   195
And so, God wot, his shield is blank enough.
His ye can have.' Then added plain Sir Torre,
'Yea, since I cannot use it, ye may have it.'
Here laugh'd the father saying, 'Fie, Sir Churl,
Is that an answer for a noble knight ?   200
Allow him ! but Lavaine, my younger here,
He is so full of lustihood, he will ride,
Joust for it, and win, and bring it in an hour,
And set it in this damsel's golden hair,
To make her thrice as wilful as before.'   205

'Nay, father, nay, good father, shame me not
Before this noble knight,' said young Lavaine,
'For nothing.   Surely I but play'd on Torre :
He seem'd so sullen, vex'd he could not go :
A jest, no more ! for, knight, the maiden dreamt   210
That some one put this diamond in her hand,
And that it was too slippery to be held,
And slipt and fell into some pool or stream,
The castle-well, belike ; and then I said
That *if* I went and *if* I fought and won it   215
(But all was jest and joke among ourselves)

Then must she keep it safelier.   All was jest.
But, father, give me leave, an if he will,
To ride to Camelot with this noble knight:
Win shall I not, but do my best to win: 220
Young as I am, yet would I do my best.'

    'So ye will grace me,' answer'd Lancelot,
Smiling a moment, 'with your fellowship
O'er these waste downs whereon I lost myself,
Then were I glad of you as guide and friend: 225
And you shall win this diamond, — as I hear,
It is a fair large diamond, — if ye may,
And yield it to this maiden, if ye will.'
'A fair large diamond,' added plain Sir Torre,
'Such be for queens, and not for simple maids.'   230
Then she, who held her eyes upon the ground,
Elaine, and heard her name so tost about,
Flush'd slightly at the slight disparagement
Before the stranger knight, who, looking at her,
Full courtly, yet not falsely, thus return'd: 235
'If what is fair be but for what is fair,
And only queens are to be counted so,
Rash were my judgment then, who deem this maid
Might wear as fair a jewel as is on earth,
Not violating the bond of like to like.'   240

    He spoke and ceased: the lily maid Elaine,
Won by the mellow voice before she look'd,
Lifted her eyes and read his lineaments.
The great and guilty love he bare the Queen,
In battle with the love he bare his lord,   245
Had marr'd his face, and mark'd it ere his time.
Another sinning on such heights with one,

The flower of all the west and all the world,
Had been the sleeker for it: but in him
His mood was often like a fiend, and rose   250
And drove him into wastes and solitudes
For agony, who was yet a living soul.
Marr'd as he was, he seem'd the goodliest man
That ever among ladies ate in hall,
And noblest, when she lifted up her eyes.   255
However marr'd, of more than twice her years,
Seam'd with an ancient swordcut on the cheek,
And bruised and bronzed, she lifted up her eyes
And loved him, with that love which was her doom.

     Then the great knight, the darling of the court,   260
Loved of the loveliest, into that rude hall
Stepp'd with all grace, and not with half disdain
Hid under grace, as in a smaller time,
But kindly man moving among his kind:
Whom they with meats and vintage of their best   265
And talk and minstrel melody entertain'd.
And much they ask'd of court and Table Round,
And ever well and readily answer'd he;
But Lancelot, when they glanced at Guinevere,
Suddenly speaking of the wordless man,   270
Heard from the Baron that, ten years before,
The heathen caught and reft him of his tongue.
'He learnt and warn'd me of their fierce design
Against my house, and him they caught and maim'd;
But I, my sons, and little daughter fled   275
From bonds or death, and dwelt among the woods
By the great river in a boatman's hut.
Dull days were those, till our good Arthur broke
The Pagan yet once more on Badon hill.'

'O there, great lord, doubtless,' Lavaine said, rapt   280
By all the sweet and sudden passion of youth
Toward greatness in its elder, 'You have fought.
O tell us — for we live apart — you know
Of Arthur's glorious wars.'   And Lancelot spoke
And answer'd him at full, as having been   285
With Arthur in the fight which all day long
Rang by the white mouth of the violent Glem ;
And in the four loud battles by the shore
Of Duglas ; that on Bassa ; then the war
That thunder'd in and out the gloomy skirts   290
Of Celidon the forest ; and again
By castle Gurnion, where the glorious King
Had on his cuirass worn our Lady's Head,
Carved of one emerald center'd in a sun
Of silver rays, that lighten'd as he breathed ;   295
And at Caerleon had he help'd his lord,
When the strong neighings of the wild white Horse
Set every gilded parapet shuddering ;
And up in Agned-Cathregonion too,
And down the waste sand-shores of Trath Treroit,   300
Where many a heathen fell ; 'and on the mount
Of Badon I myself beheld the King
Charge at the head of all his Table Round,
And all his legions crying Christ and him,
And break them ; and I saw him, after, stand   305
High on a heap of slain, from spur to plume
Red as the rising sun with heathen blood,
And seeing me, with a great voice he cried,
"They are broken, they are broken !" for the King,
However mild he seems at home, nor cares   310
For triumph in our mimic wars, the jousts —
For if his own knight cast him down, he laughs

Saying, his knights are better men than he —
Yet in this heathen war the fire of God
Fills him: I never saw his like: there lives   315
No greater leader.'

         While he utter'd this,
Low to her own heart said the lily maid,
'Save your great self, fair lord;' and when he fell
From talk of war to traits of pleasantry —
Being mirthful he, but in a stately kind —   320
She still took note that when the living smile
Died from his lips, across him came a cloud
Or melancholy severe, from which again,
Whenever in her hovering to and fro
The lily maid had striven to make him cheer,   325
There brake a sudden-beaming tenderness
Of manners and of nature: and she thought
That all was nature, all, perchance, for her.
And all night long his face before her lived,
As when a painter, poring on a face,   330
Divinely thro' all hindrance finds the man
Behind it, and so paints him that his face,
The shape and color of a mind and life,
Lives for his children, ever at its best
And fullest; so the face before her lived,   335
Dark-splendid, speaking in the silence, full
Of noble things, and held her from her sleep
Till rathe she rose, half-cheated in the thought
She needs must bid farewell to sweet Lavaine.
First as in fear, step after step, she stole   340
Down the long tower-stairs, hesitating.
Anon, she heard Sir Lancelot cry in the court,
'This shield, my friend, where is it?' and Lavaine

Pass'd inward, as she came from out the tower.
There to his proud horse Lancelot turn'd, and smooth'd 345
The glossy shoulder, humming to himself.
Half-envious of the flattering hand, she drew
Nearer and stood.   He look'd, and more amazed
Than if seven men had set upon him, saw
The maiden standing in the dewy light.   350
He had not dream'd she was so beautiful.
Then came on him a sort of sacred fear,
For silent, tho' he greeted her, she stood
Rapt on his face as if it were a God's.
Suddenly flash'd on her a wild desire,   355
That he should wear her favor at the tilt.
She braved a riotous heart in asking for it.
'Fair lord, whose name I know not — noble it is,
I well believe, the noblest — will you wear
My favor at this tourney?' 'Nay,' said he,   360
'Fair lady, since I never yet have worn
Favor of any lady in the lists.
Such is my wont, as those who know me know.'
'Yea, so,' she answer'd; 'then in wearing mine
Needs must be lesser likelihood, noble lord,   365
That those who know should know you.' And he turn'd
Her counsel up and down within his mind,
And found it true, and answer'd, 'True, my child.
Well, I will wear it: fetch it out to me:
What is it?' and she told him 'A red sleeve   370
Broider'd with pearls,' and brought it: then he bound
Her token on his helmet, with a smile
Saying, 'I never yet have done so much
For any maiden living,' and the blood
Sprang to her face and fill'd her with delight;   375
But left her all the paler, when Lavaine

LANCELOT BIDS FAREWELL TO ELAINE.

Returning brought the yet-unblazon'd shield,
His brother's; which he gave to Lancelot,
Who parted with his own to fair Elaine:
'Do me this grace, my child, to have my shield   380
In keeping till I come.' 'A grace to me,'
She answer'd, 'twice to-day. I am your squire!'
Whereat Lavaine said, laughing, 'Lily maid,
For fear our people call you lily maid
In earnest, let me bring your color back;   385
Once, twice, and thrice: now get you hence to bed;'
So kiss'd her, and Sir Lancelot his own hand,
And thus they moved away: she stay'd a minute,
Then made a sudden step to the gate, and there —
Her bright hair blown about the serious face   390
Yet rosy-kindled with her brother's kiss —
Paused by the gateway, standing near the shield
In silence, while she watch'd their arms far-off
Sparkle, until they dipp'd below the downs.
Then to her tower she climb'd, and took the shield,   395
There kept it, and so lived in fantasy.

Meanwhile the new companions pass'd away
Far o'er the long backs of the bushless downs,
To where Sir Lancelot knew there lived a knight
Not far from Camelot, now for forty years   400
A hermit, who had pray'd, labor'd and pray'd,
And ever laboring had scoop'd himself
In the white rock a chapel and a hall
On massive columns, like a shorecliff cave,
And cells and chambers: all were fair and dry;   405
The green light from the meadows underneath
Struck up and lived along the milky roofs;
And in the meadows tremulous aspen-trees

And poplars made a noise of falling showers.
And thither wending there that night they bode.   410

But when the next day broke from underground,
And shot red fire and shadows thro' the cave,
They rose, heard mass, broke fast, and rode away:
Then Lancelot saying, 'Hear, but hold my name
Hidden, you ride with Lancelot of the Lake,'   415
Abash'd Lavaine, whose instant reverence,
Dearer to true young hearts than their own praise,
But left him leave to stammer.   'Is it indeed!'
And after muttering, 'The great Lancelot.'
At last he got his breath and answered, 'One,   420
One have I seen —that other, our liege lord,
The dread Pendragon, Britain's King of kings,
Of whom the people talk mysteriously,
He will be there — then were I stricken blind
That minute, I might say that I had seen.'   425

So spake Lavaine, and when they reach'd the lists
By Camelot in the meadow, let his eyes
Run thro' the peopled gallery which half round
Lay like a rainbow fall'n upon the grass,
Until they found the clear-faced King, who sat   430
Robed in red samite, easily to be known,
Since to his crown the golden dragon clung,
And down his robe the dragon writhed in gold,
And from the carven-work behind him crept
Two dragons gilded, sloping down to make   435
Arms for his chair, while all the rest of them
Thro' knots and loops and folds innumerable
Fled ever thro' the woodwork, till they found
The new design wherein they lost themselves,

Yet with all ease, so tender was the work: 440
And, in the costly canopy o'er him set,
Blazed the last diamond of the nameless king.

  Then Lancelot answer'd young Lavaine and said,
'Me you call great: mine is the firmer seat,
The truer lance: but there is many a youth   445
Now crescent, who will come to all I am
And overcome it; and in me there dwells
No greatness, save it be some far-off touch
Of greatness to know well I am not great:
There is the man.'   And Lavaine gaped upon him   450
As on a thing miraculous, and anon
The trumpets blew; and then did either side,
They that assail'd and they that held the lists,
Set lance in rest, strike spur, suddenly move,
Meet in the midst, and there so furiously   455
Shock, that a man far-off might well perceive,
If any man that day were left afield,
The hard earth shake, and a low thunder of arms.
And Lancelot bode a little, till he saw
Which were the weaker; then he hurl'd into it   460
Against the stronger: little need to speak
Of Lancelot in his glory!   King, duke, earl,
Count, baron — whom he smote, he overthrew.

  But in the field were Lancelot's kith and kin,
Ranged with the Table Round that held the lists,   465
Strong men, and wrathful that a stranger knight
Should do and almost overdo the deeds
Of Lancelot; and one said to the other, 'Lo!
What is he?   I do not mean the force alone —
The grace and versatility of the man!   470

Is it not Lancelot?' 'When has Lancelot worn
Favor of any lady in the lists?
Not such his wont, as we that know him know.'
'How then? who then?' a fury seized them all,
A fiery family passion for the name   475
Of Lancelot, and a glory one with theirs.
They couch'd their spears and prick'd their steeds, and thus,
Their plumes driv'n backward by the wind they made
In moving, altogether down upon him
Bare, as a wild wave in the wide North-sea,   480
Green-glimmering toward the summit, bears, with all
Its stormy crests that smoke against the skies,
Down on a bark, and overbears the bark,
And him that helms it, so they overbore
Sir Lancelot and his charger, and a spear   485
Down-glancing lamed the charger, and a spear
Prick'd sharply his own cuirass, and the head
Pierced thro' his side, and there snapp'd, and remain'd.

Then Sir Lavaine did well and worshipfully;
He bore a knight of old repute to the earth,   490
And brought his horse to Lancelot where he lay.
He up the side, sweating with agony, got,
But thought to do while he might yet endure,
And being lustily holpen by the rest,
His party,—tho' it seem'd half-miracle   49?
To those he fought with,—drave his kith and kin,
And all the Table Round that held the lists,
Back to the barrier; then the trumpets blew
Proclaiming his the prize, who wore the sleeve
Of scarlet, and the pearls; and all the knights,   50?
His party, cried 'Advance and take thy prize,
The diamond;' but he answer'd 'Diamond me

No diamonds! for God's love, a little air!
Prize me no prizes, for my prize is death!
Hence will I, and I charge you, follow me not.'   505

He spoke, and vanish'd suddenly from the field
With young Lavaine into the poplar grove.
There from his charger down he slid, and sat,
Gasping to Sir Lavaine, 'Draw the lance-head;'
'Ah my sweet lord Sir Lancelot,' said Lavaine,   510
'I dread me, if I draw it, you will die.'
But he, 'I die already with it: draw —
Draw,' — and Lavaine drew, and Sir Lancelot gave
A marvellous great shriek and ghastly groan,
And half his blood burst forth, and down he sank   515
For the pure pain, and wholly swoon'd away.
Then came the hermit out and bare him in,
There stanch'd his wound; and there, in daily doubt
Whether to live or die, for many a week
Hid from the wide world's rumor by the grove   520
Of poplars with their noise of falling showers,
And ever-tremulous aspen-trees, he lay.

But on that day when Lancelot fled the lists,
His party, knights of utmost North and West,
Lords of waste marches, kings of desolate isles,   525
Came round their great Pendragon, saying to him,
'Lo, Sire, our knight, thro' whom we won the day,
Hath gone sore wounded, and hath left his prize
Untaken, crying that his prize is death.'
'Heaven hinder,' said the King, 'that such an one,   530
So great a knight as we have seen to day —
He seem'd to me another Lancelot —
Yea, twenty times I thought him Lancelot —

He must not pass uncared for. Wherefore, rise,
O Gawain, and ride forth and find the knight.　　　　53?
Wounded and wearied needs must he be near.
I charge you that you get at once to horse.
And, knights and kings, there breathes not one of you
Will deem this prize of ours is rashly given:
His prowess was too wondrous. We will do him　　　　54?
No customary honor: since the knight
Came not to us, of us to claim the prize,
Ourselves will send it after. Rise and take
This diamond, and deliver it, and return,
And bring us where he is, and how he fares,　　　　54?
And cease not from your quest until ye find.'

　　So saying, from the carven flower above,
To which it made a restless heart, he took,
And gave, the diamond: then from where he sat
At Arthur's right, with smiling face arose,　　　　55?
With smiling face and frowning heart, a Prince
In the mid might and flourish of his May,
Gawain, surnamed The Courteous, fair and strong,
And after Lancelot, Tristram, and Geraint
And Gareth, a good knight, but therewithal　　　　55?
Sir Modred's brother, and the child of Lot,
Nor often loyal to his word, and now
Wroth that the King's command to sally forth
In quest of whom he knew not, made him leave
The banquet, and concourse of knights and kings.　　　　56?

　　So all in wrath he got to horse and went;
While Arthur to the banquet, dark in mood,
Pass'd, thinking 'Is it Lancelot who hath come
Despite the wound he spake of, all for gain

Of glory, and hath added wound to wound,　　565
And ridd'n away to die?'　So fear'd the King,
And, after two days' tarriance there, return'd.
Then when he saw the Queen, embracing ask'd,
'Love, are you yet so sick?'　'Nay, lord,' she said.
'And where is Lancelot?'　Then the Queen amazed,　570
'Was he not with you? won he not your prize?'
'Nay, but one like him.'　'Why, that like was he.'
And when the King demanded how she knew,
Said, 'Lord, no sooner had ye parted from us,
Than Lancelot told me of a common talk　575
That men went down before his spear at a touch,
But knowing he was Lancelot; his great name
Conquer'd; and therefore would he hide his name
From all men, even the King, and to this end
Had made the pretext of a hindering wound,　580
That he might joust unknown of all, and learn
If his old prowess were in aught decay'd;
And added, "Our true Arthur, when he learns,
Will well allow my pretext, as for gain
Of purer glory."'

　　　　Then replied the King:　585
'Far lovelier in our Lancelot had it been,
In lieu of idly dallying with the truth,
To have trusted me as he hath trusted thee.
Surely his King and most familiar friend
Might well have kept his secret.　True, indeed,　590
Albeit I know my knights fantastical,
So fine a fear in our large Lancelot
Must needs have moved my laughter: now remains
But little cause for laughter: his own kin—
Ill news, my Queen, for all who love him, this!—　595

His kith and kin, not knowing, set upon him
So that he went sore wounded from the field:
Yet good news too: for goodly hopes are mine
That Lancelot is no more a lonely heart.
He wore, against his wont, upon his helm   600
A sleeve of scarlet, broider'd with great pearls,
Some gentle maiden's gift.'

                              'Yea, lord,' she said,
'Thy hopes are mine,' and saying that, she choked,
And sharply turn'd about to hide her face,
Pass'd to her chamber, and there flung herself   605
Down on the great King's couch, and writhed upon it,
And clench'd her fingers till they bit the palm,
And shriek'd out, 'Traitor,' to the unhearing wall,
Then flash'd into wild tears, and rose again,
And moved about her palace, proud and pale.   610

    Gawain the while thro' all the region round
Rode with his diamond, wearied of the quest,
Touch'd at all points, except the poplar grove,
And came at last, tho' late, to Astolat:
Whom glittering in enamell'd arms the maid   615
Glanced at, and cried, 'What news from Camelot, lord?
What of the knight with the red sleeve?' 'He won.'
'I knew it,' she said. 'But parted from the jousts
Hurt in the side,' whereat she caught her breath;
Thro' her own side she felt the sharp lance go;   620
Thereon she smote her hand: wellnigh she swoon'd:
And, while he gazed wonderingly at her, came
The Lord of Astolat out, to whom the Prince
Reported who he was, and on what quest
Sent, that he bore the prize and could not find   62-
The victor, but had ridd'n a random round

To seek him, and had wearied of the search.
To whom the Lord of Astolat, 'Bide with us,
And ride no more at random, noble Prince!
Here was the knight, and here he left a shield;   630
This will he send or come for; furthermore,
Our son is with him; we shall hear anon.
Needs must we hear.'   To this the courteous Prince
Accorded with his wonted courtesy,
Courtesy with a touch of traitor in it,   635
And stay'd; and cast his eyes on fair Elaine:
Where could be found face daintier? then her shape
From forehead down to foot, perfect — again
From foot to forehead exquisitely turn'd:
'Well — if I bide, lo! this wild flower for me!'   640
And oft they met among the garden yews,
And there he set himself to play upon her
With sallying wit, free flashes from a height
Above her, graces of the court, and songs,
Sighs, and slow smiles, and golden eloquence   645
And amorous adulation, till the maid
Rebell'd against it, saying to him, 'Prince,
O loyal nephew of our noble King,
Why ask you not to see the shield he left,
Whence you might learn his name? Why slight your King,
And lose the quest he sent you on, and prove   651
No surer than our falcon yesterday,
Who lost the hern we slipp'd her at, and went
To all the winds?' 'Nay, by mine head,' said he,
I lose it, as we lose the lark in heaven,   655
O damsel, in the light of your blue eyes;
But an ye will it let me see the shield.'
And when the shield was brought, and Gawain saw
Sir Lancelot's azure lions, crown'd with gold,

Ramp in the field, he smote his thigh, and mock'd: 666
'Right was the King! our Lancelot! that true man!'
'And right was I,' she answer'd merrily, 'I,
Who dream'd my knight the greatest knight of all.'
'And if *I* dream'd,' said Gawain, 'that you love
This greatest knight, your pardon! lo, ye know it!   665
Speak therefore; shall I waste myself in vain?'
Full simple was her answer, 'What know I?
My brethren have been all my fellowship;
And I, when often they have talk'd of love,
Wish'd it had been my mother, for they talk'd,   670
Meseem'd, of what they knew not; so myself—
I know not if I know what true love is,
But if I know, then, if I love not him,
I know there is none other I can love.'
'Yea, by God's death,' said he, 'ye love him well,   675
But would not, knew ye what all others know,
And whom he loves.'   'So be it,' cried Elaine,
And lifted her fair face and moved away:
But he pursued her, calling, 'Stay a little!
One golden minute's grace! he wore your sleeve: 680
Would he break faith with one I may not name?
Must our true man change like a leaf at last?
Nay—like enow: why then, far be it from me
To cross our mighty Lancelot in his loves!
And, damsel, for I deem you know full well   685
Where your great knight is hidden, let me leave
My quest with you; the diamond also: here!
For if you love, it will be sweet to give it;
And if he love, it will be sweet to have it
From your own hand; and whether he love or not,   690
A diamond is a diamond.   Fare you well
A thousand times!—a thousand times farewell!

Yet, if he love, and his love hold, we two
May meet at court hereafter: there, I think,
So ye will learn the courtesies of the court,   695
We two shall know each other.'

              Then he gave,
And slightly kiss'd the hand to which he gave,
The diamond, and all wearied of the quest
Leapt on his horse, and carolling as he went
A true-love ballad, lightly rode away.   700

   Thence to the court he pass'd; there told the King
What the King knew, 'Sir Lancelot is the knight.'
And added, 'Sire, my liege, so much I learnt;
But fail'd to find him, tho' I rode all round
The region: but I lighted on the maid   705
Whose sleeve he wore; she loves him; and to her,
Deeming our courtesy is the truest law,
I gave the diamond: she will render it;
For by mine head she knows his hiding-place.'

   The seldom-frowning King frown'd, and replied,   710
'Too courteous truly! ye shall go no more
On quest of mine, seeing that ye forget
Obedience is the courtesy due to kings.'

   He spake and parted. Wroth, but all in awe,
For twenty strokes of the blood, without a word,   715
Linger'd that other, staring after him;
Then shook his hair, strode off, and buzz'd abroad
About the maid of Astolat, and her love.
All ears were prick'd at once, all tongues were loosed:
'The maid of Astolat loves Sir Lancelot,   720
Sir Lancelot loves the maid of Astolat.'

Some read the King's face, some the Queen's, and all
Had marvel what the maid might be, but most
Predoom'd her as unworthy.   One old dame
Came suddenly on the Queen with the sharp news.   725
She, that had heard the noise of it before,
But sorrowing Lancelot should have stoop'd so low,
Marr'd her friend's aim with pale tranquillity.
So ran the tale like fire about the court,
Fire in dry stubble a nine-days' wonder flared: 730
Till even the knights at banquet twice or thrice
Forgot to drink to Lancelot and the Queen,
And pledging Lancelot and the lily maid
Smiled at each other, while the Queen, who sat
With lips severely placid, felt the knot   735
Climb in her throat, and with her feet unseen
Crush'd the wild passion out against the floor
Beneath the banquet, where the meats became
As wormwood, and she hated all who pledged.

But far away the maid in Astolat,   740
Her guiltless rival, she that ever kept
The one-day-seen Sir Lancelot in her heart,
Crept to her father, while he mused alone,
Sat on his knee, stroked his gray face and said,
'Father, you call me wilful, and the fault   745
Is yours who let me have my will, and now,
Sweet father, will you let me lose my wits?'
'Nay,' said he, 'surely.'   'Wherefore, let me hence,'
She answer'd, 'and find out our dear Lavaine.'
'Ye will not lose your wits for dear Lavaine: 750
Bide,' answer'd he: 'we needs must hear anon
Of him, and of that other.'   'Ay,' she said,
'And of that other, for I needs must hence

And find that other, wheresoe'er he be,
And with mine own hand give his diamond to him,   755
Lest I be found as faithless in the quest
As yon proud Prince who left the quest to me.
Sweet father, I behold him in my dreams
Gaunt as it were the skeleton of himself,
Death-pale, for lack of gentle maiden's aid.   760
The gentler-born the maiden, the more bound,
My father, to be sweet and serviceable
To noble knights in sickness, as ye know
When these have worn their tokens : let me hence
I pray you.'   Then her father nodding said,   765
'Ay, ay, the diamond : wit ye well, my child,
Right fain were I to learn this knight were whole,
Being our greatest : yea, and you must give it —
And sure I think this fruit is hung too high
For any mouth to gape for save a queen's —   770
Nay, I mean nothing : so then, get you gone,
Being so very wilful you must go.'

Lightly, her suit allow'd, she slipp'd away,
And while she made her ready for her ride,
Her father's latest word humm'd in her ear,   775
'Being so very wilful you must go.'
And changed itself and echo'd in her heart,
'Being so very wilful you must die.'
But she was happy enough and shook it off,
As we shake off the bee that buzzes at us ;   780
And in her heart she answer'd it and said,
'What matter, so I help him back to life ?'
Then far away with good Sir Torre for guide
Rode o'er the long backs of the bushless downs
To Camelot, and before the city-gates   785

Came on her brother with a happy face
Making a roan horse caper and curvet
For pleasure all about a field of flowers:
Whom when she saw, 'Lavaine,' she cried, 'Lavaine,
How fares my lord Sir Lancelot?'   He amazed,   790
'Torre and Elaine! why here?   Sir Lancelot!
How know ye my lord's name is Lancelot?'
But when the maid had told him all her tale,
Then turn'd Sir Torre, and being in his moods
Left them, and under the strange-statued gate,   795
Where Arthur's wars were render'd mystically,
Pass'd up the still rich city to his kin,
His own far blood, which dwelt at Camelot;
And her, Lavaine across the poplar grove
Led to the caves: there first she saw the casque   800
Of Lancelot on the wall: her scarlet sleeve,
Tho' carved and cut, and half the pearls away,
Stream'd from it still; and in her heart she laugh'd,
Because he had not loosed it from his helm,
But meant once more perchance to tourney in it.   805
And when they gain'd the cell wherein he slept,
His battle-writhen arms and mighty hands
Lay naked on the wolfskin, and a dream
Of dragging down his enemy made them move.
Then she that saw him lying unsleek, unshorn,   810
Gaunt as it were the skeleton of himself,
Utter'd a little tender dolorous cry.
The sound not wonted in a place so still
Woke the sick knight, and while he roll'd his eyes
Yet blank from sleep, she started to him, saying,   815
'Your prize the diamond sent you by the King:'
His eyes glisten'd: she fancied 'Is it for me?'
And when the maid had told him all the tale

Of King and Prince, the diamond sent, the quest
Assign'd to her not worthy of it, she knelt   820
Full lowly by the corners of his bed,
And laid the diamond in his open hand.
Her face was near, and as we kiss the child
That does the task assign'd, he kiss'd her face;
At once she slipp'd like water to the floor.   825
'Alas,' he said, 'your ride hath wearied you.
Rest must you have.' 'No rest for me,' she said;
'Nay, for near you, fair lord, I am at rest.'
What might she mean by that? his large black eyes,
Yet larger thro' his leanness, dwelt upon her,   830
Till all her heart's sad secret blazed itself
In the heart's colors on her simple face;
And Lancelot look'd and was perplex'd in mind,
And being weak in body said no more;
But did not love the color; woman's love,   835
Save one, he not regarded, and so turn'd
Sighing, and feign'd a sleep until he slept.

  Then rose Elaine and glided thro' the fields,
And pass'd beneath the weirdly-sculptured gates
Far up the dim rich city to her kin;   840
There bode the night: but woke with dawn, and pass'd
Down thro' the dim rich city to the fields,
Thence to the cave: so day by day she pass'd
In either twilight ghost-like to and fro
Gliding, and every day she tended him,   845
And likewise many a night: and Lancelot
Would, tho' he call'd his wound a little hurt
Whereof he should be quickly whole, at times
Brain-feverous in his heat and agony, seem
Uncourteous, even he: but the meek maid   850

Sweetly forbore him ever, being to him
Meeker than any child to a rough nurse,
Milder than any mother to a sick child,
And never woman yet, since man's first fall,
Did kindlier unto man, but her deep love   855
Upbore her; till the hermit, skill'd in all
The simples and the science of that time,
Told him that her fine care had saved his life.
And the sick man forgot her simple blush,
Would call her friend and sister, sweet Elaine,   860
Would listen for her coming and regret
Her parting step, and held her tenderly,
And loved her with all love except the love
Of man and woman when they love their best,
Closest and sweetest, and had died the death   865
In any knightly fashion for her sake.
And peradventure had he seen her first
She might have made this and that other world
Another world for the sick man; but now
The shackles of an old love straiten'd him,   870
His honor rooted in dishonor stood,
And faith unfaithful kept him falsely true.

Yet the great knight in his mid-sickness made
Full many a holy vow and pure resolve.
These, as but born of sickness, could not live: 875
For when the blood ran lustier in him again,
Full often the bright image of one face,
Making a treacherous quiet in his heart,
Dispersed his resolution like a cloud.
Then if the maiden, while that ghostly grace   880
Beam'd on his fancy, spoke, he answer'd not,
Or short and coldly, and she knew right well

What the rough sickness meant, but what this meant
She knew not, and the sorrow dimm'd her sight,
And drave her ere her time across the fields   885
Far into the rich city, where alone
She murmur'd, 'Vain, in vain: it cannot be.
He will not love me: how then? must I die?'
Then as a little helpless innocent bird,
That has but one plain passage of few notes,   890
Will sing the simple passage o'er and o'er
For all an April morning till the ear
Wearies to hear it, so the simple maid
Went half the night repeating, 'Must I die?'
And now to right she turn'd, and now to left,   895
And found no ease in turning or in rest;
And 'Him or death,' she mutter'd, 'death or him,'
Again and like a burthen, 'Him or death.'

    But when Sir Lancelot's deadly hurt was whole,
To Astolat returning rode the three.   900
There morn by morn, arraying her sweet self
In that wherein she deem'd she look'd her best,
She came before Sir Lancelot, for she thought
'If I be loved, these are my festal robes,
If not, the victim's flowers before he fall.'   905
And Lancelot ever press'd upon the maid
That she should ask some goodly gift of him
For her own self or hers: 'and do not shun
To speak the wish most near to your true heart;
Such service have ye done me, that I make   910
My will of yours, and Prince and Lord am I
In mine own land, and what I will I can.'
Then like a ghost she lifted up her face,
But like a ghost without the power to speak.

And Lancelot saw that she withheld her wish.   913
And bode among them yet a little space
Till he should learn it; and one morn it chanced
He found her in among the garden yews,
And said, 'Delay no longer, speak your wish,
Seeing I go to-day:' then out she brake: 920
'Going? and we shall never see you more.
And I must die for want of one bold word.'
'Speak: that I live to hear,' he said, 'is yours.'
Then suddenly and passionately she spoke:
'I have gone mad.   I love you: let me die.'   925
'Ah, sister,' answer'd Lancelot, 'what is this?'
And innocently extending her white arms,
'Your love,' she said, 'your love — to be your wife.'
And Lancelot answered, 'Had I chosen to wed,
I had been wedded earlier, sweet Elaine: 930
But now there never will be wife of mine.'
'No, no,' she cried, 'I care not to be wife,
But to be with you still, to see your face,
To serve you, and to follow you thro' the world.'
And Lancelot answer'd, 'Nay, the world, the world,   935
All ear and eye, with such a stupid heart
To interpret ear and eye, and such a tongue
To blare its own interpretation — nay,
Full ill then should I quit your brother's love,
And your good father's kindness.'   And she said,   940
'Not to be with you, not to see your face —
Alas for me then, my good days are done.'
'Nay, noble maid,' he answer'd, 'ten times nay!
This is not love: but love's first flash in youth,
Most common: yea, I know it of mine own self: 943
And you yourself will smile at your own self
Hereafter, when you yield your flower of life

To one more fitly yours, not thrice your age:
And then will I, for true you are and sweet
Beyond mine old belief in womanhood,   950
More specially should your good knight be poor,
Endow you with broad land and territory
Even to the half my realm beyond the seas,
So that would make you happy: furthermore,
Even to the death, as tho' ye were my blood,   955
In all your quarrels will I be your knight.
This will I do, dear damsel, for your sake,
And more than this I cannot.'

                While he spoke
She neither blush'd nor shook, but deathly-pale
Stood grasping what was nearest, then replied: 960
'Of all this will I nothing;' and so fell,
And thus they bore her swooning to her tower.

   Then spake, to whom thro' those black walls of yew
Their talk had pierced, her father: 'Ay, a flash,
I fear me, that will strike my blossom dead.   965
Too courteous are ye, fair Lord Lancelot.
I pray you, use some rough discourtesy
To blunt or break her passion.'

                Lancelot said,
'That were against me: what I can I will;'
And there that day remain'd, and toward even   970
Sent for his shield: full meekly rose the maid,
Stripp'd off the case, and gave the naked shield;
Then, when she heard his horse upon the stones,
Unclasping flung the casement back, and look'd
Down on his helm, from which her sleeve had gone.   975
And Lancelot knew the little clinking sound;

And she by tact of love was well aware
Then Lancelot knew that she was looking at him.
And yet he glanced not up, nor waved his hand,
Nor bade farewell, but sadly rode away.   980
This was the one discourtesy that he used.

So in her tower alone the maiden sat :
His very shield was gone ; only the case,
Her own poor work, her empty labor, left.
But still she heard him, still his picture form'd   985
And grew between her and the pictured wall.
Then came her father, saying in low tones,
'Have comfort,' whom she greeted quietly.
Then came her brethren saying, 'Peace to thee,
Sweet sister,' whom she answer'd with all calm.   990
But when they left her to herself again,
Death, like a friend's voice from a distant field
Approaching thro' the darkness, call'd ; the owls
Wailing had power upon her, and she mix'd
Her fancies with the sallow-rifted glooms   995
Of evening and the moanings of the wind.

And in those days she made a little song,
And call'd her song 'The Song of Love and Death,'
And sang it : sweetly could she make and sing.

'Sweet is true love tho' given in vain, in vain ;   1000
And sweet is death who puts an end to pain :
I know not which is sweeter, no, not I.

'Love, art thou sweet ? then bitter death must be :
Love, thou art bitter ; sweet is death to me.
O Love, if death be sweeter, let me die   1005

'Sweet love, that seems not made to fade away,
Sweet death, that seems to make us loveless clay,
I know not which is sweeter, no, not I.

'I fain would follow love, if that could be;
I needs must follow death, who calls for me;   1010
Call and I follow, I follow! let me die.'

High with the last line scaled her voice, and this,
All in a fiery dawning wild with wind
That shook her tower, the brothers heard, and thought
With shuddering, 'Hark the Phantom of the house   1015
That ever shrieks before a death,' and call'd
The father, and all three in hurry and fear
Ran to her, and lo! the blood-red light of dawn
Flared on her face, she shrilling, 'Let me die!'

As when we dwell upon a word we know,   1020
Repeating, till the word we know so well
Becomes a wonder, and we know not why,
So dwelt the father on her face, and thought
'Is this Elaine?' till back the maiden fell,
Then gave a languid hand to each, and lay,   1025
Speaking a still good-morrow with her eyes.
At last she said, 'Sweet brothers, yesternight
I seem'd a curious little maid again,
As happy as when we dwelt among the woods,
And when ye used to take me with the flood   1030
Up the great river in the boatman's boat.
Only ye would not pass beyond the cape
That has the poplar on it: there ye fix'd
Your limit, oft returning with the tide.

And yet I cried because ye would not pass   1035
Beyond it, and far up the shining flood
Until we found the palace of the King.
And yet ye would not; but this night I dream'd
That I was all alone upon the flood,
And then I said, "Now shall I have my will:"   1040
And there I woke, but still the wish remain'd.
So let me hence, that I may pass at last
Beyond the poplar and far up the flood,
Until I find the palace of the King.
There will I enter in among them all,   1045
And no man there will dare to mock at me;
But there the fine Gawain will wonder at me,
And there the great Sir Lancelot muse at me;
Gawain, who bad a thousand farewells to me,
Lancelot, who coldly went, nor bad me one;   1050
And there the King will know me and my love,
And there the Queen herself will pity me,
And all the gentle court will welcome me,
And after my long voyage I shall rest!'

    'Peace,' said her father, 'O my child, ye seem   1055
Light-headed, for what force is yours to go
So far, being sick? and wherefore would ye look
On this proud fellow again, who scorns us all?'

    Then the rough Torre began to heave and move
And bluster into stormy sobs and say,   1060
'I never loved him: an I meet with him,
I care not howsoever great he be,
Then will I strike at him and strike him down,
Give me good fortune, I will strike him dead,
For this discomfort he hath done the house.'   1065

To whom the gentle sister made reply,
'Fret not yourself, dear brother, nor be wroth,
Seeing it is no more Sir Lancelot's fault
Not to love me, than it is mine to love
Him of all men who seems to me the highest.' 1076

'Highest?' the father answer'd, echoing 'highest?'
(He meant to break the passion in her) 'nay,
Daughter, I know not what you call the highest;
But this I know, for all the people know it,
He loves the Queen, and in an open shame: 1078
And she returns his love in open shame;
If this be high, what is it to be low?'

Then spake the lily maid of Astolat:
'Sweet father, all too faint and sick am I
For anger: these are slanders: never yet 1083
Was noble man but made ignoble talk.
He makes no friend who never made a foe.
But now it is my glory to have loved
One peerless, without stain; so let me pass,
My father, howsoe'er I seem to you, 1085
Not all unhappy, having loved God's best
And greatest, tho' my love had no return:
Yet, seeing you desire your child to live,
Thanks, but you work against your own desire;
For if I could believe the things you say 1090
I should but die the sooner; wherefore cease,
Sweet father, and bid call the ghostly man
Hither, and let me shrive me clean, and die.'

So when the ghostly man had come and gone,
She, with a face bright as for sin forgiven, 1095

Besought Lavaine to write as she devised
A letter, word for word; and when he ask'd
'Is it for Lancelot, is it for my dear lord?
Then will I bear it gladly;' she replied,
'For Lancelot and the Queen and all the world,   1100
But I myself must bear it.'   Then he wrote
The letter she devised; which being writ
And folded, 'O sweet father, tender and true,
Deny me not,' she said — 'ye never yet
Denied my fancies — this, however strange,   1105
My latest: lay the letter in my hand
A little ere I die, and close the hand
Upon it; I shall guard it even in death.
And when the heat is gone from out my heart,
Then take the little bed on which I died   1110
For Lancelot's love, and deck it like the Queen's
For richness, and me also like the Queen
In all I have of rich, and lay me on it.
And let there be prepared a chariot-bier
To take me to the river, and a barge   1115
Be ready on the river, clothed in black.
I go in state to court to meet the Queen.
There surely I shall speak for mine own self,
And none of you can speak for me so well.
And therefore let our dumb old man alone   1120
Go with me, he can steer and row, and he
Will guide me to that palace, to the doors.'

She ceased: her father promised; whereupon
She grew so cheerful that they deem'd her death
Was rather in the fantasy than the blood.   1125
But ten slow mornings pass'd, and on the eleventh
Her father laid the letter in her hand,

Torre and Lavaine Bid Farewell to the Body of Elaine

And closed the hand upon it, and she died.
So that day there was dole in Astolat.

But when the next sun brake from underground,   1130
Then, those two brethren slowly with bent brows
Accompanying, the sad chariot-bier
Pass'd like a shadow thro' the field, that shone
Full-summer, to that stream whereon the barge,
Pall'd all its length in blackest samite, lay.   1135
There sat the lifelong creature of the house,
Loyal, the dumb old servitor, on deck,
Winking his eyes, and twisted all his face.
So those two brethren from the chariot took
And on the black decks laid her in her bed,   1140
Set in her hand a lily, o'er her hung
The silken case with braided blazonings,
And kiss'd her quiet brows, and saying to her
'Sister, farewell for ever,' and again
'Farewell, sweet sister,' parted all in tears.   1145
Then rose the dumb old servitor, and the dead,
Oar'd by the dumb, went upward with the flood—
In her right hand the lily, in her left
The letter—all her bright hair streaming down—
And all the coverlid was cloth of gold   1150
Drawn to her waist, and she herself in white
All but her face, and that clear-featured face
Was lovely, for she did not seem as dead,
But fast asleep, and lay as tho' she smiled.

That day Sir Lancelot at the palace craved   1155
Audience of Guinevere, to give at last
The price of half a realm, his costly gift,

Hard-won and hardly won with bruise and blow,
With deaths of others, and almost his own,
The nine-years-fought-for diamonds: for he saw   1160
One of her house, and sent him to the Queen
Bearing his wish, whereto the Queen agreed
With such and so unmoved a majesty
She might have seem'd her statue, but that he,
Low-drooping till he wellnigh kiss'd her feet   1165
For loyal awe, saw with a sidelong eye
The shadow of some piece of pointed lace,
In the Queen's shadow, vibrate on the walls,
And parted, laughing in his courtly heart.

All in an oriel on the summer side,   1170
Vine-clad, of Arthur's palace toward the stream,
They met, and Lancelot kneeling utter'd, 'Queen,
Lady, my liege, in whom I have my joy,
Take, what I had not won except for you,
These jewels, and make me happy, making them   1175
An armlet for the roundest arm on earth,
Or necklace for a neck to which the swan's
Is tawnier than her cygnet's: these are words:
Your beauty is your beauty, and I sin
In speaking, yet O grant my worship of it   1180
Words, as we grant grief tears.   Such sin in words,
Perchance, we both can pardon: but, my Queen,
I hear of rumors flying thro' your court.
Our bond, as not the bond of man and wife,
Should have in it an absoluter trust   1185
To make up that defect: let rumors be:
When did not rumors fly? these, as I trust
That you trust me in your own nobleness,
I may not well believe that you believe.'

While thus he spoke, half turn'd away, the Queen 1190
Brake from the vast oriel-embowering vine
Leaf after leaf, and tore, and cast them off,
Till all the place whereon she stood was green:
Then, when he ceased, in one cold passive hand
Received at once and laid aside the gems 1195
There on a table near her, and replied:

'It may be, I am quicker of belief
Than you believe me, Lancelot of the Lake.
Our bond is not the bond of man and wife.
This good is in it, whatsoe'er of ill, 1200
It can be broken easier. I for you
This many a year have done despite and wrong
To one whom ever in my heart of hearts
I did acknowledge nobler. What are these?
Diamonds for me! they had been thrice their worth 1205
Being your gift, had you not lost your own.
To loyal hearts the value of all gifts
Must vary as the giver's. Not for me!
For her! for your new fancy. Only this
Grant me, I pray you: have your joys apart. 1210
I doubt not that however changed, you keep
So much of what is graceful: and myself
Would shun to break those bounds of courtesy
In which as Arthur's Queen I move and rule:
So cannot speak my mind. An end to this: 1215
A strange one! yet I take it with Amen.
So pray you, add my diamonds to her pearls;
Deck her with these; tell her, she shines me down:
An armlet for an arm to which the Queen's
Is haggard, or a necklace for a neck 1220
O as much fairer — as a faith once fair

Was richer than these diamonds — hers, not mine —
Nay, by the mother of our Lord himself,
Or hers or mine, mine now to work my will —
She shall not have them.'

       Saying which she seized, 1225
And, thro' the casement standing wide for heat,
Flung them, and down they flash'd, and smote the stream.
Then from the smitten surface flash'd, as it were,
Diamonds to meet them, and they pass'd away.
Then while Sir Lancelot leant, in half disdain 1230
At love, life, all things, on the window ledge,
Close underneath his eyes, and right across
Where these had fallen, slowly pass'd the barge
Whereon the lily maid of Astolat
Lay smiling, like a star in blackest night. 1235

 But the wild Queen, who saw not, burst away
To weep and wail in secret; and the barge,
On to the palace-doorway sliding, paused.
There two stood arm'd, and kept the door; to whom,
All up the marble stair, tier over tier, 1240
Were added mouths that gaped, and eyes that ask'd
'What is it?' but that oarsman's haggard face,
As hard and still as is the face that men
Shape to their fancy's eye from broken rocks
On some cliff-side, appall'd them, and they said, 1245
'He is enchanted, cannot speak — and she,
Look how she sleeps — the Fairy Queen, so fair!
Yea, but how pale! what are they? flesh and blood?
Or come to take the King to Fairyland?
For some do hold our Arthur cannot die, 1250
But that he passes into Fairyland.'

While thus they babbled of the King, the King
Came girt with knights: then turn'd the tongueless man
From the half-face to the full eye, and rose
And pointed to the damsel, and the doors.   1255
So Arthur bade the meek Sir Percivale
And pure Sir Galahad to uplift the maid;
And reverently they bore her into hall.
Then came the fine Gawain and wonder'd at her,
And Lancelot later came and mused at her,   1260
And last the Queen herself, and pitied her:
But Arthur spied the letter in her hand,
Stoop'd, took, brake seal, and read it; this was all:

'Most noble lord, Sir Lancelot of the Lake,
I, sometime call'd the maid of Astolat,   1265
Come, for you left me taking no farewell,
Hither, to take my last farewell of you.
I loved you, and my love had no return,
And therefore my true love has been my death.
And therefore to our Lady Guinevere,   1270
And to all other ladies, I make moan.
Pray for my soul, and yield me burial.
Pray for my soul thou too, Sir Lancelot,
As thou art a knight peerless.'

                              Thus he read;
And ever in the reading, lords and dames   1275
Wept, looking often from his face who read
To hers which lay so silent, and at times,
So touch'd were they, half-thinking that her lips,   .
Who had devised the letter, moved again.

Then freely spoke Sir Lancelot to them all: 1280
'My lord liege Arthur, and all ye that hear,

Know that for this most gentle maiden's death
Right heavy am I; for good she was and true,
But loved me with a love beyond all love
In women, whomsoever I have known.   1285
Yet to be loved makes not to love again;
Not at my years, however it hold in youth.
I swear by truth and knighthood that I gave
No cause, not willingly, for such a love:
To this I call my friends in testimony,   1290
Her brethren, and her father who himself
Besought me to be plain and blunt, and use,
To break her passion, some discourtesy
Against my nature; what I could, I did.
I left her and I bade her no farewell;   1295
Tho' had I dreamt the damsel would have died,
I might have put my wits to some rough use,
And help'd her from herself.'

                              Then said the Queen
(Sea was her wrath, yet working after storm),
'Ye might at least have done her so much grace,   1300
Fair lord, as would have help'd her from her death.'
He raised his head, their eyes met and hers fell,
He adding,

                    'Queen, she would not be content
Save that I wedded her, which could not be.
Then might she follow me thro' the world, she ask'd;   1305
It could not be.   I told her that her love
Was but the flash of youth, would darken down
To rise hereafter in a stiller flame
Toward one more worthy of her — then would I,
More specially were he she wedded poor,   1310
Estate them with large land and territory

In mine own realm beyond the narrow seas,
To keep them in all joyance: more than this
I could not; this she would not, and she died.'

He pausing, Arthur answer'd, 'O my knight,   1315
It will be to thy worship, as my knight,
And mine, as head of all our Table Round,
To see that she be buried worshipfully.'

So toward that shrine which then in all the realm
Was richest, Arthur leading, slowly went   1320
The marshall'd Order of their Table Round,
And Lancelot sad beyond his wont, to see
The maiden buried, not as one unknown,
Nor meanly, but with gorgeous obsequies,
And mass, and rolling music, like a queen.   1325
And when the knights had laid her comely head
Low in the dust of half-forgotten kings,
Then Arthur spake among them, 'Let her tomb
Be costly, and her image thereupon,
And let the shield of Lancelot at her feet   1330
Be carven, and her lily in her hand.
And let the story of her dolorous voyage
For all true hearts be blazon'd on her tomb
In letters gold and azure!' which was wrought
Thereafter; but when now the lords and dames   1335
And people, from the high door streaming, brake
Disorderly, as homeward each, the Queen,
Who mark'd Sir Lancelot where he moved apart,
Drew near, and sigh'd in passing, 'Lancelot,
Forgive me; mine was jealousy in love.'   1340
He answer'd with his eyes upon the ground,
'That is love's curse; pass on, my Queen, forgiven.'

But Arthur, who beheld his cloudy brows,
Approach'd him, and with full affection said,

'Lancelot, my Lancelot, thou in whom I have   1345
Most joy and most affiance, for I know
What thou hast been in battle by my side,
And many a time have watch'd thee at the tilt
Strike down the lusty and long practised knight,
And let the younger and unskill'd go by   1350
To win his honor and to make his name,
And loved thy courtesies and thee, a man
Made to be loved; but now I would to God,
Seeing the homeless trouble in thine eyes,
Thou couldst have loved this maiden, shaped, it seems, 1355
By God for thee alone, and from her face,
If one may judge the living by the dead,
Delicately pure and marvellously fair,
Who might have brought thee, now a lonely man
Wifeless and heirless, noble issue, sons   1360
Born to the glory of thy name and fame,
My knight, the great Sir Lancelot of the Lake.'

Then answer'd Lancelot, 'Fair she was, my King,
Pure, as you ever wish your knights to be.
To doubt her fairness were to want an eye,   1365
To doubt her pureness were to want a heart —
Yea, to be loved, if what is worthy love
Could bind him, but free love will not be bound.'

'Free love, so bound, were freest,' said the King.
'Let love be free; free love is for the best: 1370
And, after heaven, on our dull side of death,
What should be best, if not so pure a love

Clothed in so pure a loveliness? yet thee
She failed to bind, tho' being, as I think,
Unbound as yet, and gentle, as I know.'   137**5**

    And Lancelot answer'd nothing, but he went,
And at the inrunning of a little brook
Sat by the river in a cove, and watch'd
The high reed wave, and lifted up his eyes
And saw the barge that brought her moving down,   1380
Far-off, a blot upon the stream, and said
Low in himself, 'Ah, simple heart and sweet,
Ye loved me, damsel, surely with a love
Far tenderer than my Queen's. Pray for thy soul?
Ay, that will I. Farewell too — now at last —   1385
Farewell, fair lily. "Jealousy in love?"
Not rather dead love's harsh heir, jealous pride?
Queen, if I grant the jealousy as of love,
May not your crescent fear for name and fame
Speak, as it waxes, of a love that wanes?   1390
Why did the King dwell on my name to me?
Mine own name shames me, seeming a reproach,
Lancelot, whom the Lady of the Lake
Caught from his mother's arms — the wondrous one
Who passes thro' the vision of the night —   1395
She chanted snatches of mysterious hymns
Heard on the winding waters, eve and morn
She kiss'd me saying, "Thou art fair, my child,
As a king's son," and often in her arms
She bare me, pacing on the dusky mere.   1400
Would she had drown'd me in it, where'er it be!
For what am I? what profits me my name
Of greatest knight? I fought for it, and have it:
Pleasure to have it, none; to lose it, pain;

Now grown a part of me: but what use in it?   1408
To make man worse by making my sin known?
Or sin seem less, the sinner seeming great?
Alas for Arthur's greatest knight, a man
Not after Arthur's heart!   I needs must break
These bonds that so defame me: not without   1410
She wills it: would I, if she will'd it? nay,
Who knows? but if I would not, then may God,
I pray him, send a sudden Angel down
To seize me by the hair and bear me far,
And fling me deep in that forgotten mere,   1415
Among the tumbled fragments of the hills.'

So groan'd Sir Lancelot in remorseful pain,
Not knowing he should die a holy man.

SIR GALAHAD.

THE HOLY GRAIL.

FROM noiseful arms, and acts of prowess done
In tournament or tilt, Sir Percivale,
Whom Arthur and his knighthood call'd The Pure,
Had pass'd into the silent life of prayer,
Praise, fast, and alms; and leaving for the cowl   5
The helmet in an abbey far away
From Camelot, there, and not long after, died.

And one, a fellow-monk among the rest,
Ambrosius, loved him much beyond the rest,
And honor'd him, and wrought into his heart   10
A way by love that waken'd love within,
To answer that which came: and as they sat
Beneath a world-old yew-tree, darkening half
The cloisters, on a gustful April morn
That puff'd the swaying branches into smoke   15
Above them, ere the summer when he died,
The monk Ambrosius question'd Percivale:

"O brother, I have seen this yew-tree smoke,
Spring after spring, for half a hundred years:
For never have I known the world without,   20
Nor ever stray'd beyond the pale: but thee,
When first thou camest — such a courtesy
Spake thro' the limbs and in the voice — I knew
For one of those who eat in Arthur's hall;
For good ye are and bad, and like to coins,   25
Some true, some light, but every one of you
Stamp'd with the image of the King; and now
Tell me, what drove thee from the Table Round,
My brother? was it earthly passion crost?"

"Nay," said the knight; "for no such passion mine.   30
But the sweet vision of the Holy Grail
Drove me from all vainglories, rivalries,
And earthly heats that spring and sparkle out
Among us in the jousts, while women watch
Who wins, who falls; and waste the spiritual strength   35
Within us, better offer'd up to Heaven."

To whom the monk: "The Holy Grail!— I trust
We are green in Heaven's eyes; but here too much
We moulder — as to things without I mean —
Yet one of your own knights, a guest of ours,   40
Told us of this in our refectory,
But spake with such a sadness and so low
We heard not half of what he said.   What is it?
The phantom of a cup that comes and goes?"

"Nay, monk! what phantom?" answer'd Percivale.   45
"The cup, the cup itself, from which our Lord
Drank at the last sad supper with his own.
This, from the blessed land of Aromat —
After the day of darkness, when the dead
Went wandering o'er Moriah — the good saint,   50
Arimathæan Joseph, journeying brought
To Glastonbury, where the winter thorn
Blossoms at Christmas, mindful of our Lord.
And there awhile it bode; and if a man
Could touch or see it, he was heal'd at once,   55
By faith, of all his ills.   But then the times
Grew to such evil that the holy cup
Was caught away to Heaven, and disappear'd."

To whom the monk: "From our old books I know
That Joseph came of old to Glastonbury,   60

And there the heathen Prince, Arviragus,
Gave him an isle of marsh whereon to build;
And there he built with wattles from the marsh
A little lonely church in days of yore,
For so they say, these books of ours, but seem   65
Mute of this miracle, far as I have read.
But who first saw the holy thing to-day?"

"A woman," answer'd Percivale, "a nun,
And one no further off in blood from me
Than sister; and if ever holy maid   70
With knees of adoration wore the stone,
A holy maid; tho' never maiden glow'd,
But that was in her earlier maidenhood,
With such a fervent flame of human love,
Which being rudely blunted, glanced and shot   75
Only to holy things; to prayer and praise
She gave herself, to fast and alms.   And yet,
Nun as she was, the scandal of the Court,
Sin against Arthur and the Table Round,
And the strange sound of an adulterous race,   80
Across the iron grating of her cell
Beat, and she pray'd and fasted all the more.

"And he to whom she told her sins, or what
Her all but utter whiteness held for sin,
A man well-nigh a hundred winters old,   85
Spake often with her of the Holy Grail,
A legend handed down thro' five or six,
And each of these a hundred winters old,
From our Lord's time.   And when King Arthur made
His Table Round, and all men's hearts became   90
Clean for a season, surely he had thought

That now the Holy Grail would come again;
But sin broke out.   Ah, Christ, that it would come,
And heal the world of all their wickedness!
'O Father!' ask'd the maiden, 'might it come   95
To me by prayer and fasting?'   'Nay,' said he,
'I know not, for thy heart is pure as snow.'
And so she pray'd and fasted, till the sun
Shone, and the wind blew, thro' her, and I thought
She might have risen and floated when I saw her.   100

  "For on a day she sent to speak with me.
And when she came to speak, behold her eyes
Beyond my knowing of them, beautiful,
Beyond all knowing of them, wonderful,
Beautiful in the light of holiness.   105
And 'O my brother Percivale,' she said,
'Sweet brother, I have seen the Holy Grail:
For, waked at dead of night, I heard a sound
As of a silver horn from o'er the hills
Blown, and I thought, "It is not Arthur's use   110
To hunt by moonlight;" and the slender sound
As from a distance beyond distance grew
Coming upon me — O never harp nor horn,
Nor ought we blow with breath, or touch with hand,
Was like that music as it came; and then   115
Stream'd thro' my cell a cold and silver beam,
And down the long beam stole the Holy Grail,
Rose-red with beatings in it, as if alive,
Till all the white walls of my cell were dyed
With rosy colors leaping on the wall;   120
And then the music faded, and the Grail
Past, and the beam decay'd, and from the walls
The rosy quiverings died into the night.

PERCIVALE'S SISTER.

So now the Holy Thing is here again
Among us, brother, fast thou too and pray,   125
And tell thy brother knights to fast and pray,
That so perchance the vision may be seen
By thee and those, and all the world be heal'd.'

  "Then leaving the pale nun, I spake of this
To all men; and myself fasted and pray'd   130
Always, and many among us many a week
Fasted and pray'd even to the uttermost,
Expectant of the wonder that would be.

  "And one there was among us, ever moved
Among us in white armor, Galahad.   135
'God make thee good as thou art beautiful,'
Said Arthur, when he dubb'd him knight; and none,
In so young youth, was ever made a knight
Till Galahad; and this Galahad, when he heard
My sister's vision, fill'd me with amaze;   140
His eyes became so like her own, they seem'd
Hers, and himself her brother more than I.

  "Sister or brother none had he; but some
Call'd him a son of Lancelot, and some said
Begotten by enchantment — chatterers they,   145
Like birds of passage piping up and down,
That gape for flies — we know not whence they come
For when was Lancelot wanderingly lewd?

  "But she, the wan sweet maiden, shore away
Clean from her forehead all that wealth of hair   150
Which made a silken mat-work for her feet;
And out of this she plaited broad and long
A strong sword-belt, and wove with silver thread

And crimson in the belt a strange device,
A crimson grail within a silver beam;   155
And saw the bright boy-knight, and bound it on him,
Saying, 'My knight, my love, my knight of heaven,
O thou, my love, whose love is one with mine,
I, maiden, round thee, maiden, bind my belt.
Go forth, for thou shalt see what I have seen,   160
And break thro' all, till one will crown thee king
Far in the spiritual city:' and as she spake
She sent the deathless passion in her eyes
Thro' him, and made him hers, and laid her mind
On him, and he believed in her belief.   165

     " Then came a year of miracle: O brother,
In our great hall there stood a vacant chair,
Fashion'd by Merlin ere he past away,
And carven with strange figures; and in and out
The figures, like a serpent, ran a scroll   170
Of letters in a tongue no man could read.
And Merlin call'd it 'The Siege perilous,'
Perilous for good and ill; 'for there,' he said,
'No man could sit but he should lose himself:'
And once by misadvertence Merlin sat   175
In his own chair, and so was lost; but he,
Galahad, when he heard of Merlin's doom,
Cried, 'If I lose myself, I save myself!'

     " Then on a summer night it came to pass,
While the great banquet lay along the hall,   180
That Galahad would sit down in Merlin's chair.

     " And all at once, as there we sat, we heard
A cracking and a riving of the roofs,

And rending, and a blast, and overhead
Thunder, and in the thunder was a cry. 185
And in the blast there smote along the hall
A beam of light seven times more clear than day:
And down the long beam stole the Holy Grail
All over cover'd with a luminous cloud,
And none might see who bare it, and it past. 190
But every knight beheld his fellow's face
As in a glory, and all the knights arose,
And staring each at other like dumb men
Stood, till I found a voice and sware a vow.

"I sware a vow before them all, that I, 195
Because I had not seen the Grail, would ride
A twelvemonth and a day in quest of it,
Until I found and saw it, as the nun
My sister saw it; and Galahad sware the vow,
And good Sir Bors, our Lancelot's cousin, sware, 200
And Lancelot sware, and many among the knights,
And Gawain sware, and louder than the rest."

Then spake the monk Ambrosius, asking him,
"What said the King?   Did Arthur take the vow?"

"Nay, for my lord," said Percivale, "the King, 205
Was not in hall: for early that same day,
Scaped thro' a cavern from a bandit hold,
An outraged maiden sprang into the hall
Crying on help: for all her shining hair
Was smear'd with earth, and either milky arm 210
Red-rent with hooks of bramble, and all she wore
Torn as a sail that leaves the rope is torn
In tempest: so the King arose and went

To smoke the scandalous hive of those wild bees
That made such honey in his realm. Howbeit   215
Some little of this marvel he too saw,
Returning o'er the plain that then began
To darken under Camelot; whence the King
Look'd up, calling aloud, ' Lo, there ! the roofs
Of our great hall are roll'd in thunder-smoke !   220
Pray Heaven, they be not smitten by the bolt.'
For dear to Arthur was that hall of ours,
As having there so oft with all his knights
Feasted, and as the stateliest under heaven.

"O brother, had you known our mighty hall,   225
Which Merlin built for Arthur long ago !
For all the sacred mount of Camelot,
And all the dim rich city, roof by roof,
Tower after tower, spire beyond spire,
By grove, and garden-lawn, and rushing brook,   230
Climbs to the mighty hall that Merlin built.
And four great zones of sculpture, set betwixt
With many a mystic symbol, gird the hall :
And in the lowest beasts are slaying men,
And in the second men are slaying beasts,   235
And on the third are warriors, perfect men,
And on the fourth are men with growing wings,
And over all one statue in the mould
Of Arthur, made by Merlin, with a crown,
And peak'd wings pointed to the Northern Star.   240
And eastward fronts the statue, and the crown
And both the wings are made of gold, and flame
At sunrise till the people in far fields,
Wasted so often by the heathen hordes,
Behold it, crying, ' We have still a King.'   245

VISION OF THE GRAIL.

" And, brother, had you known our hall within,
Broader and higher than any in all the lands !
Where twelve great windows blazon Arthur's wars,
And all the light that falls upon the board
Streams thro' the twelve great battles of our King.   250
Nay, one there is, and at the eastern end,
Wealthy with wandering lines of mount and mere,
Where Arthur finds the brand Excalibur.
And also one to the west, and counter to it,
And blank : and who shall blazon it ? when and how ? — 255
O there, perchance, when all our wars are done,
The brand Excalibur will be cast away.

" So to this hall full quickly rode the King,
In horror lest the work by Merlin wrought,
Dreamlike, should on the sudden vanish, wrapt   260
In unremorseful folds of rolling fire.
And in he rode and up I glanced, and saw
The golden dragon sparkling over all :
And many of those who burnt the hold, their arms   264
Hack'd and their foreheads grimed with smoke, and sear'd,
Follow'd, and in among bright faces, ours,
Full of the vision, prest : and then the King
Spake to me, being nearest, ' Percivale,'
(Because the hall was all in tumult — some
Vowing, and some protesting), ' what is this ? '   270

" O brother, when I told him what had chanced,
My sister's vision, and the rest, his face
Darken'd, as I have seen it more than once,
When some brave deed seem'd to be done in vain,
Darken ; and ' Woe is me, my knights,' he cried,   275
' Had I been here, ye had not sworn the vow.'

Bold was mine answer, 'Had thyself been here,
My King, thou wouldst have sworn.'　'Yea, yea,' said he,
'Art thou so bold and hast not seen the Grail?'

"'Nay, lord, I heard the sound, I saw the light,　　　280
But since I did not see the Holy Thing,
I sware a vow to follow it till I saw.'

"Then when he ask'd us, knight by knight, if any
Had seen it, all their answers were as one:
'Nay, lord, and therefore have we sworn our vows.'　　　285

"'Lo now,' said Arthur, 'have ye seen a cloud?
What go ye into the wilderness to see?'

"Then Galahad on the sudden, and in a voice
Shrilling along the hall to Arthur call'd,
'But I, Sir Arthur, saw the Holy Grail,　　　290
I saw the Holy Grail and heard a cry —
"O Galahad, and O Galahad, follow me."'

"'Ah, Galahad, Galahad,' said the King, 'for such
As thou art is the vision, not for these.
The holy nun and thou have seen a sign —　　　295
Holier is none, my Percivale, than she —
A sign to maim this Order which I made.
But ye, that follow but the leader's bell'
(Brother, the King was hard upon his knights)
'Taliessin is our fullest throat of song,　　　300
And one hath sung and all the dumb will sing.
Lancelot is Lancelot, and hath overborne
Five knights at once, and every younger knight,
Unproven, holds himself as Lancelot,
Till overborne by one, he learns — and ye,　　　305

What are ye?   Galahads? — no, nor Percivales'
(For thus it pleased the King to range me close
After Sir Galahad); 'nay,' said he, ' but men
With strength and will to right the wrong'd, of power
To lay the sudden heads of violence flat,   310
Knights that in twelve great battles splash'd and dyed
The strong White Horse in his own heathen blood —
But one hath seen, and all the blind will see.
Go, since your vows are sacred, being made:
Yet — for ye know the cries of all my realm   315
Pass thro' this hall — how often, O my knights,
Your places being vacant at my side,
This chance of noble deeds will come and go
Unchallenged, while ye follow wandering fires
Lost in the quagmire!   Many of you, yea most,   320
Return no more: ye think I show myself
Too dark a prophet: come now, let us meet
The morrow morn once more in one full field
Of gracious pastime, that once more the King,
Before ye leave him for this Quest, may count   325
The yet-unbroken strength of all his knights,
Rejoicing in that Order which he made.'

  " So when the sun broke next from under ground,
All the great table of our Arthur closed
And clash'd in such a tourney and so full,   330
So many lances broken — never yet
Had Camelot seen the like, since Arthur came ;
And I myself and Galahad, for a strength
Was in us from the vision, overthrew
So many knights that all the people cried,   335
And almost burst the barriers in their heat,
Shouting, ' Sir Galahad and Sir Percivale!'

" But when the next day brake from under ground —
O brother, had you known our Camelot,
Built by old kings, age after age, so old   340
The King himself had fears that it would fall,
So strange, and rich, and dim; for where the roofs
Totter'd toward each other in the sky,
Met foreheads all along the street of those
Who watch'd us pass; and lower, and where the long   345
Rich galleries, lady-laden, weigh'd the necks
Of dragons clinging to the crazy walls,
Thicker than drops from thunder, showers of flowers
Fell as we past; and men and boys astride
On wyvern, lion, dragon, griffin, swan,   350
At all the corners, named us each by name,
Calling ' God speed!' but in the ways below
The knights and ladies wept, and rich and poor
Wept, and the King himself could hardly speak
For grief, and all in middle street the Queen,   355
Who rode by Lancelot, wail'd and shriek'd aloud,
'This madness has come on us for our sins.'
So to the Gate of the three Queens we came,
Where Arthur's wars are render'd mystically,
And thence departed every one his way.   360

" And I was lifted up in heart, and thought
Of all my late-shown prowess in the lists,
How my strong lance had beaten down the knights,
So many and famous names; and never yet
Had Heaven appear'd so blue, nor earth so green,   365
For all my blood danced in me, and I knew
That I should light upon the Holy Grail.

"Thereafter, the dark warning of our King,
That most of us would follow wandering fires.

Came like a driving gloom across my mind.   370
Then every evil word I had spoken once,
And every evil thought I had thought of old,
And every evil deed I ever did,
Awoke and cried, 'This Quest is not for thee.'
And lifting up mine eyes, I found myself   375
Alone, and in a land of sand and thorns,
And I was thirsty even unto death;
And I, too, cried, 'This Quest is not for thee.'

  "And on I rode, and when I thought my thirst
Would slay me, saw deep lawns, and then a brook,   380
With one sharp rapid, where the crisping white
Play'd ever back upon the sloping wave,
And took both ear and eye; and o'er the brook
Were apple-trees, and apples by the brook
Fallen, and on the lawns. 'I will rest here,'   385
I said, 'I am not worthy of the Quest;'
But even while I drank the brook, and ate
The goodly apples, all these things at once
Fell into dust, and I was left alone,
And thirsting, in a land of sand and thorns   390

  "And then behold a woman at a door
Spinning; and fair the house whereby she sat,
And kind the woman's eyes and innocent,
And all her bearing gracious; and she rose
Opening her arms to meet me, as who should say,   395
'Rest here;' but when I touch'd her, lo! she, too,
Fell into dust and nothing, and the house
Became no better than a broken shed,
And in it a dead babe; and also this
Fell into dust, and I was left alone.   400

" And on I rode, and greater was my thirst.
Then flash'd a yellow gleam across the world,
And where it smote the plowshare in the field,
The plowman left his plowing, and fell down
Before it ; where it glitter'd on her pail   405
The milkmaid left her milking, and fell down
Before it, and I knew not why, but thought
' The sun is rising,' tho' the sun had risen.
Then was I ware of one that on me moved
In golden armor with a crown of gold   410
About a casque all jewels ; and his horse
In golden armor jewell'd everywhere :
And on the splendor came, flashing me blind ;
And seem'd to me the Lord of all the world,
Being so huge.   But when I thought he meant   415
To crush me, moving on me, lo ! he, too,
Open'd his arms to embrace me as he came,
And up I went and touch'd him, and he, too,
Fell into dust, and I was left alone
And wearying in a land of sand and thorns.   420

" And I rode on and found a mighty hill,
And on the top, a city wall'd : the spires
Prick'd with incredible pinnacles into heaven.
And by the gateway stirr'd a crowd ; and these
Cried to me climbing, ' Welcome, Percivale !   425
Thou mightiest and thou purest among men !'
And glad was I and clomb, but found at top
No man, nor any voice.   And thence I past
Far thro' a ruinous city, and I saw
That man had once dwelt there ; but there I found   430
Only one man of an exceeding age.
'Where is that goodly company,' said I,

'That so cried out upon me?' and he had
Scarce any voice to answer, and yet gasp'd,
'Whence and what art thou?' and even as he spoke   435
Fell into dust, and disappear'd, and I
Was left alone once more, and cried in grief,
'Lo, if I find the Holy Grail itself
And touch it, it will crumble into dust.'

  " And thence I dropt into a lowly vale,   440
Low as the hill was high, and where the vale
Was lowest, found a chapel, and thereby
A holy hermit in a hermitage,
To whom I told my phantoms, and he said:

  " ' O son, thou hast not true humility,   445
The highest virtue, mother of them all;
For when the Lord of all things made Himself
Naked of glory for His mortal change,
" Take thou my robe," she said, " for all is thine,"
And all her form shone forth with sudden light   450
So that the angels were amazed, and she
Follow'd Him down, and like a flying star
Led on the gray-hair'd wisdom of the east;
But her thou hast not known: for what is this
Thou thoughtest of thy prowess and thy sins?   455
Thou hast not lost thyself to save thyself
As Galahad.'   When the hermit made an end,
In silver armor suddenly Galahad shone
Before us, and against the chapel door
Laid lance, and enter'd, and we knelt in prayer.   460
And there the hermit slaked my burning thirst,
And at the sacring of the mass I saw
The holy elements alone; but he,

'Saw ye no more?　I, Galahad, saw the Grail,
The Holy Grail, descend upon the shrine:　　　　465
I saw the fiery face as of a child
That smote itself into the bread, and went;
And hither am I come; and never yet
Hath what thy sister taught me first to see,
This Holy Thing, fail'd from my side, nor come　　470
Cover'd, but moving with me night and day,
Fainter by day, but always in the night
Blood-red, and sliding down the blacken'd marsh
Blood-red, and on the naked mountain top
Blood-red, and in the sleeping mere below　　　　475
Blood-red.　And in the strength of this I rode,
Shattering all evil customs everywhere,
And past thro' Pagan realms, and made them mine,
And clash'd with Pagan hordes, and bore them down,
And broke thro' all, and in the strength of this　　480
Come victor.　But my time is hard at hand,
And hence I go; and one will crown me king
Far in the spiritual city; and come thou, too,
For thou shalt see the vision when I go.'

　"While thus he spake, his eye, dwelling on mine,　485
Drew me, with power upon me, till I grew
One with him, to believe as he believed.
Then, when the day began to wane, we went.

　"There rose a hill that none but man could climb,
Scarr'd with a hundred wintry water-courses —　　490
Storm at the top, and when we gain'd it, storm
Round us and death; for every moment glanced
His silver arms and gloom'd: so quick and thick
The lightnings here and there to left and right

THE PASSING OF GALAHAD.

Struck, till the dry old trunks about us, dead,   495
Yea, rotten with a hundred years of death,
Sprang into fire : and at the base we found
On either hand, as far as eye could see,
A great black swamp and of an evil smell,
Part black, part whiten'd with the bones of men,   500
Not to be crost, save that some ancient king
Had built a way, where, link'd with many a bridge,
A thousand piers ran into the great Sea.
And Galahad fled along them bridge by bridge,
And every bridge as quickly as he crost   505
Sprang into fire and vanish'd, tho' I yearn'd
To follow ; and thrice above him all the heavens
Open'd and blazed with thunder such as seem'd
Shoutings of all the sons of God : and first
At once I saw him far on the great Sea,   510
In silver-shining armor starry-clear ;
And o'er his head the Holy Vessel hung
Clothed in white samite or a luminous cloud.
And with exceeding swiftness ran the boat,
If boat it were — I saw not whence it came.   515
And when the heavens open'd and blazed again
Roaring, I saw him like a silver star —
And had he set the sail, or had the boat
Become a living creature clad with wings ?
And o'er his head the Holy Vessel hung   520
Redder than any rose, a joy to me,
For now I knew the veil had been withdrawn.
Then in a moment when they blazed again
Opening, I saw the least of little stars
Down on the waste, and straight beyond the star   525
I saw the spiritual city and all her spires
And gateways in a glory like one pearl —

No larger, tho' the goal of all the saints —
Strike from the sea; and from the star there shot
A rose-red sparkle to the city, and there   530
Dwelt, and I knew it was the Holy Grail,
Which never eyes on earth again shall see.
Then fell the floods of heaven drowning the deep.
And how my feet recrost the deathful ridge
No memory in me lives; but that I touch'd   535
The chapel-doors at dawn I know; and thence
Taking my war-horse from the holy man,
Glad that no phantom vext me more, return'd
To whence I came, the gate of Arthur's wars."

    "O brother," ask'd Ambrosius, — "for in sooth   540
These ancient books — and they would win thee — teem,
Only I find not there this Holy Grail,
With miracles and marvels like to these,
Not all unlike; which oftentime I read,
Who read but on my breviary with ease,   545
Till my head swims; and then go forth and pass
Down to the little thorpe that lies so close,
And almost plaster'd like a martin's nest
To these old walls — and mingle with our folk;
And knowing every honest face of theirs   550
As well as ever shepherd knew his sheep,
And every homely secret in their hearts,
Delight myself with gossip and old wives,
And ills and aches, and teethings, lyings-in,
And mirthful sayings, children of the place,   555
That have no meaning half a league away:
Or lulling random squabbles when they rise,
Chafferings and chatterings at the market-cross,
Rejoice, small man, in this small world of mine.

Yea, even in their hens and in their eggs — 560
O brother, saving this Sir Galahad,
Came ye on none but phantoms in your quest,
No man, no woman?"

Then Sir Percivale:
"All men, to one so bound by such a vow,
And women were as phantoms. O, my brother, 565
Why wilt thou shame me to confess to thee
How far I falter'd from my quest and vow?
For after I had lain so many nights,
A bedmate of the snail and eft and snake,
In grass and burdock, I was changed to wan 570
And meagre, and the vision had not come;
And then I chanced upon a goodly town
With one great dwelling in the middle of it;
Thither I made, and there was I disarm'd
By maidens each as fair as any flower: 575
But when they led me into hall, behold,
The Princess of that castle was the one,
Brother, and that one only, who had ever
Made my heart leap; for when I moved of old
A slender page about her father's hall, 580
And she a slender maiden, all my heart
Went after her with longing: yet we twain
Had never kiss'd a kiss, or vow'd a vow.
And now I came upon her once again,
And one had wedded her, and he was dead, 585
And all his land and wealth and state were hers.
And while I tarried, every day she set
A banquet richer than the day before
By me; for all her longing and her will
Was toward me as of old; till one fair morn, 590

I walking to and fro beside a stream
That flash'd across her orchard underneath
Her castle-walls, she stole upon my walk,
And calling me the greatest of all knights,
Embraced me, and so kiss'd me the first time,   595
And gave herself and all her wealth to me.
Then I remember'd Arthur's warning word,
That most of us would follow wandering fires,
And the Quest faded in my heart.   Anon,
The heads of all her people drew to me,   600
With supplication both of knees and tongue:
' We have heard of thee : thou art our greatest knight,
Our Lady says it, and we well believe :
Wed thou our Lady, and rule over us,
And thou shalt be as Arthur in our land.'   605
O me, my brother ! but one night my vow
Burnt me within, so that I rose and fled,
But wail'd and wept, and hated mine own self,
And ev'n the Holy Quest, and all but her ;
Then after I was join'd with Galahad   610
Cared not for her, nor anything upon earth."

     Then said the monk, " Poor men, when yule is cold,
Must be content to sit by little fires.
And this am I, so that ye care for me
Ever so little ; yea, and blest be Heaven   615
That brought thee here to this poor house of ours
Where all the brethren are so hard, to warm
My cold heart with a friend : but O the pity
To find thine own first love once more — to hold,
Hold her a wealthy bride within thine arms,   620
Or all but hold, and then — cast her aside,
Foregoing all her sweetness, like a weed.

For we that want the warmth of double life,
We that are plagued with dreams of something sweet
Beyond all sweetness in a life so rich, —   625
Ah, blessed Lord, I speak too earthlywise,
Seeing I never stray'd beyond the cell,
But live like an old badger in his earth,
With earth about him everywhere, despite
All fast and penance.   Saw ye none beside,   630
None of your knights?"

                                "Yea so," said Percivale
"One night my pathway swerving east, I saw
The pelican on the casque of our Sir Bors
All in the middle of the rising moon:
And toward him spurr'd, and hail'd him, and he me,   635
And each made joy of either; then he ask'd
'Where is he? hast thou seen him — Lancelot? — Once,'
Said good Sir Bors, 'he dash'd across me — mad,
And maddening what he rode: and when I cried,
"Ridest thou then so hotly on a quest   640
So holy," Lancelot shouted, "Stay me not!
I have been the sluggard, and I ride apace,
For now there is a lion in the way."
So vanish'd.'

                "Then Sir Bors had ridden on
Softly, and sorrowing for our Lancelot,   645
Because his former madness, once the talk
And scandal of our table, had return'd;
For Lancelot's kith and kin so worship him
That ill to him is ill to them; to Bors
Beyond the rest: he well had been content   650
Not to have seen, so Lancelot might have seen,

The Holy Cup of healing; and, indeed,
Being so crowded with his grief and love,
Small heart was his after the Holy Quest:
If God would send the vision, well: if not,   655
The Quest and he were in the hands of Heaven.

    "And then, with small adventure met, Sir Bors
Rode to the lonest tract of all the realm,
And found a people there among their crags,
Our race and blood, a remnant that were left   660
Paynim amid their circles, and the stones
They pitch up straight to heaven: and their wise men
Were strong in that old magic which can trace
The wandering of the stars, and scoff'd at him
And this high Quest as at a simple thing: 665
Told him he follow'd — almost Arthur's words —
A mocking fire : 'what other fire than he,
Whereby the blood beats, and the blossom blows,
And the sea rolls, and all the world is warm'd?'
And when his answer chafed them, the rough crowd,   670
Hearing he had a difference with their priests,
Seized him, and bound and plunged him into a cell
Of great piled stones; and lying bounden there
In darkness thro' innumerable hours
He heard the hollow-ringing heavens sweep   675
Over him till by miracle — what else? —
Heavy as it was, a great stone slipt and fell
Such as no wind could move: and thro' the gap
Glimmer'd the streaming scud : then came a night
Still as the day was loud; and thro' the gap   680
The seven clear stars of Arthur's Table Round —
For, brother, so one night, because they roll
Thro' such a round in heaven, we named the stars,

Rejoicing in ourselves and in our King —
And these, like bright eyes of familiar friends,   685
In on him shone: 'And then to me, to me,'
Said good Sir Bors, 'beyond all hopes of mine,
Who scarce had pray'd or ask'd it for myself —
Across the seven clear stars — O grace to me —
In color like the fingers of a hand   690
Before a burning taper, the sweet Grail
Glided and past, and close upon it peal'd
A sharp quick thunder.'   Afterwards a maid,
Who kept our holy faith among her kin
In secret, entering, loosed and let him go."   695

    To whom the monk: "And I remember now
That pelican on the casque. Sir Bors it was
Who spake so low and sadly at our board;
And mighty reverent at our grace was he:
A square-set man and honest; and his eyes,   700
An out-door sign of all the warmth within,
Smiled with his lips — a smile beneath a cloud,
But heaven had meant it for a sunny one:
Ay, ay, Sir Bors, who else?   But when ye reach'd
The city, found ye all your knights return'd,   705
Or was there sooth in Arthur's prophecy,
Tell me, and what said each, and what the King?"

    Then answer'd Percivale: "And that can I,
Brother, and truly; since the living words
Of so great men as Lancelot and our King   710
Pass not from door to door and out again,
But sit within the house.   O, when we reach'd
The city, our horses stumbling as they trode
On heaps of ruin, hornless unicorns,

Crack'd basilisks, and splinter'd cockatrices,   715
And shatter'd talbots, which had left the stones
Raw, that they fell from, brought us to the hall.

"And there sat Arthur on the daïs-throne,
And those that had gone out upon the Quest,
Wasted and worn, and but a tithe of them,   720
And those that had not, stood before the King,
Who, when he saw me, rose, and bad me hail,
Saying, 'A welfare in thine eye reproves
Our fear of some disastrous chance for thee
On hill, or plain, at sea, or flooding ford.   725
So fierce a gale made havoc here of late
Among the strange devices of our kings;
Yea, shook this newer, stronger hall of ours,
And from the statue Merlin moulded for us
Half-wrench'd a golden wing; but now — the Quest,   730
This vision — hast thou seen the Holy Cup,
That Joseph brought of old to Glastonbury?'

"So when I told him all thyself hast heard,
Ambrosius, and my fresh but fixt resolve
To pass away into the quiet life,   735
He answer'd not, but, sharply turning, ask'd
Of Gawain, 'Gawain, was this Quest for thee?'

"'Nay, lord,' said Gawain, 'not for such as I.
Therefore I communed with a saintly man,
Who made me sure the Quest was not for me;   740
For I was much awearied of the Quest:
But found a silk pavilion in a field,
And merry maidens in it; and then this gale
Tore my pavilion from the tenting-pin,

The Return from the Quest.

And blew my merry maidens all about   745
With all discomfort; yea, and but for this,
My twelvemonth and a day were pleasant to me.'

  "He ceased; and Arthur turn'd to whom at first
He saw not, for Sir Bors, on entering, push'd
Athwart the throng to Lancelot, caught his hand,   750
Held it, and there, half-hidden by him, stood,
Until the King espied him, saying to him,
'Hail, Bors! if ever loyal man and true
Could see it, thou hast seen the Grail;' and Bors,
'Ask me not, for I may not speak of it: 755
I saw it;' and the tears were in his eyes.

  "Then there remain'd but Lancelot, for the rest
Spake but of sundry perils in the storm;
Perhaps, like him of Cana in Holy Writ,
Our Arthur kept his best until the last;   760
'Thou, too, my Lancelot,' ask'd the King, 'my friend,
Our mightiest, hath this Quest avail'd for thee?'

  "'Our mightiest!' answer'd Lancelot, with a groan;
'O King!'—and when he paused, methought I spied
A dying fire of madness in his eyes—   765
'O King, my friend, if friend of thine I be,
Happier are those that welter in their sin,
Swine in the mud, that cannot see for slime,
Slime of the ditch: but in me lived a sin
So strange, of such a kind, that all of pure,   770
Noble, and knightly in me twined and clung
Round that one sin, until the wholesome flower
And poisonous grew together, each as each,
Not to be pluck'd asunder; and when thy knights

Sware, I sware with them only in the hope   775
That could I touch or see the Holy Grail
They might be pluck'd asunder.   Then I spake
To one most holy saint, who wept and said,
That save they could be pluck'd asunder, all
My quest were but in vain; to whom I vow'd   780
That I would work according as he will'd
And forth I went, and while I yearn'd and strove
To tear the twain asunder in my heart,
My madness came upon me as of old,
And whipt me into waste fields far away;   785
There was I beaten down by little men,
Mean knights, to whom the moving of my sword
And shadow of my spear had been enow
To scare them from me once; and then I came
All in my folly to the naked shore,   790
Wide flats, where nothing but coarse grasses grew;
But such a blast, my King, began to blow,
So loud a blast along the shore and sea,
Ye could not hear the waters for the blast,
Tho' heapt in mounds and ridges all the sea   795
Drove like a cataract, and all the sand
Swept like a river, and the clouded heavens
Were shaken with the motion and the sound.
And blackening in the sea-foam sway'd a boat
Half-swallow'd in it, anchor'd with a chain;   800
And in my madness to myself I said,
"I will embark and I will lose myself,
And in the great sea wash away my sin."
I burst the chain, I sprang into the boat.
Seven days I drove along the dreary deep,   805
And with me drove the moon and all the stars;
And the wind fell and on the seventh night

I heard the shingle grinding in the surge,
And felt the boat shock earth, and looking up,
Behold, the enchanted towers of Carbonek, 810
A castle like a rock upon a rock,
With chasm-like portals open to the sea,
And steps that met the breaker! there was none
Stood near it but a lion on each side
That kept the entry, and the moon was full. 815
Then from the boat I leapt, and up the stairs.
There drew my sword. With sudden flaring manes
Those two great beasts rose upright like a man,
Each gript a shoulder, and I stood between;
And, when I would have smitten them, heard a voice, 820
"Doubt not, go forward; if thou doubt, the beasts
Will tear thee piecemeal." Then with violence
The sword was dash'd from out my hand, and fell.
And up into the sounding hall I past;
But nothing in the sounding hall I saw, 825
No bench nor table, painting on the wall
Or shield of knight; only the rounded moon
Thro' the tall oriel on the rolling sea.
But always in the quiet house I heard,
Clear as a lark, high o'er me as a lark, 830
A sweet voice singing in the topmost tower
To the eastward: up I climb'd a thousand steps
With pain: as in a dream I seem'd to climb
For ever: at the last I reach'd a door,
A light was in the crannies, and I heard, 835
"Glory and joy and honor to our Lord
And to the Holy Vessel of the Grail."
Then in my madness I essay'd the door;
It gave; and thro' a stormy glare, a heat
As from a seventimes-heated furnace, I, 840

Blasted and burnt, and blinded as I was,
With such a fierceness that I swoon'd away —
O, yet methought I saw the Holy Grail,
All pall'd in crimson samite, and around
Great angels, awful shapes, and wings and eyes.   845
And but for all my madness and my sin,
And then my swooning, I had sworn I saw
That which I saw; but what I saw was veil'd
And cover'd; and this Quest was not for me.'

"So speaking, and here ceasing, Lancelot left   850
The hall long silent, till Sir Gawain — nay,
Brother, I need not tell thee foolish words, —
A reckless and irreverent knight was he,
Now bolden'd by the silence of his King, —
Well, I will tell thee: 'O King, my liege,' he said,   855
'Hath Gawain fail'd in any quest of thine?
When have I stinted stroke in foughten field?
But as for thine, my good friend Percivale,
Thy holy nun and thou have driven men mad,
Yea, made our mightiest madder than our least.   860
But by mine eyes and by mine ears I swear,
I will be deafer than the blue-eyed cat,
And thrice as blind as any noonday owl,
To holy virgins in their ecstasies,
Henceforward.'

                    "'Deafer,' said the blameless King,   865
'Gawain, and blinder unto holy things
Hope not to make thyself by idle vows,
Being too blind to have desire to see.
But if indeed there came a sign from heaven,
Blessed are Bors, Lancelot and Percivale.   870

For these have seen according to their sight.
For every fiery prophet in old times,
And all the sacred madness of the bard,
When God made music thro' them, could but speak
His music by the framework and the chord;   875
And as ye saw it ye have spoken truth.

"'Nay — but thou errest, Lancelot: never yet
Could all of true and noble in knight and man
Twine round one sin, whatever it might be,
With such a closeness, but apart there grew,   880
Save that he were the swine thou spakest of,
Some root of knighthood and pure nobleness;
Whereto see thou, that it may bear its flower.

"'And spake I not too truly, O my knights?
Was I too dark a prophet when I said   885
To those who went upon the Holy Quest,
That most of them would follow wandering fires,
Lost in the quagmire? — lost to me and gone,
And left me gazing at a barren board,
And a lean Order — scarce return'd a tithe —   890
And out of those to whom the vision came
My greatest hardly will believe he saw;
Another hath beheld it afar off,
And leaving human wrongs to right themselves,
Cares but to pass into the silent life.   895
And one hath had the vision face to face,
And now his chair desires him here in vain,
However they may crown him otherwhere.

"'And some among you held, that if the King
Had seen the sight he would have sworn the vow: 900

Not easily, seeing that the King must guard
That which he rules, and is but as the hind
To whom a space of land is given to plow,
Who may not wander from the allotted field
Before his work be done; but, being done,   905
Let visions of the night or of the day
Come, as they will; and many a time they come,
Until this earth he walks on seems not earth,
This light that strikes his eyeball is not light,
This air that smites his forehead is not air   910
But vision — yea, his very hand and foot —
In moments when he feels he cannot die,
And knows himself no vision to himself,
Nor the high God a vision, nor that One
Who rose again: ye have seen what ye have seen.'   915

"So spake the King: I knew not all he meant."

THE PASSING OF ARTHUR.

THAT story which the bold Sir Bedivere,
First made and latest left of all the knights,
Told, when the man was no more than a voice
In the white winter of his age, to those
With whom he dwelt, new faces, other minds.   5

For on their march to westward, Bedivere,
Who slowly paced among the slumbering host,
Heard in his tent the moanings of the King:

'I found Him in the shining of the stars,
I mark'd Him in the flowering of His fields,   10
But in His ways with men I find Him not.
I waged His wars, and now I pass and die.
O me! for why is all around us here
As if some lesser god had made the world,
But had not force to shape it as he would,   15
Till the High God behold it from beyond,
And enter it, and make it beautiful?
Or else as if the world were wholly fair,
But that these eyes of men are dense and dim,
And have not power to see it as it is: 20
Perchance, because we see not to the close; —
For I, being simple, thought to work His will,
And have but stricken with the sword in vain;
And all whereon I lean'd in wife and friend
Is traitor to my peace, and all my realm   25
Reels back into the beast, and is no more.
My God, thou hast forgotten me in my death:
Nay — God my Christ — I pass but shall not die.'

Then, ere that last weird battle in the west,
There came on Arthur sleeping, Gawain kill'd   30
In Lancelot's war, the Ghost of Gawain blown
Along a wandering wind, and past his ear
Went shrilling, 'Hollow, hollow all delight!
Hail, King! to-morrow thou shalt pass away.
Farewell! there is an isle of rest for thee.   35
And I am blown along a wandering wind,
And hollow, hollow, hollow all delight.'
And fainter onward, like wild birds that change
Their season in the night and wail their way
From cloud to cloud, down the long wind the dream   40
Shrill'd; but in going mingled with dim cries
Far in the moonlit haze among the hills,
As of some lonely city sack'd by night,
When all is lost, and wife and child with wail
Pass to new lords; and Arthur woke and call'd,   45
'Who spake? A dream. O light upon the wind,
Thine, Gawain, was the voice — are these dim cries
Thine? or doth all that haunts the waste and wild
Mourn, knowing it will go along with me?'

This heard the bold Sir Bedivere and spake: 50
'O me, my King, let pass whatever will,
Elves, and the harmless glamour of the field;
But in their stead thy name and glory cling
To all high places like a golden cloud
For ever: but as yet thou shalt not pass.   55
Light was Gawain in life, and light in death
Is Gawain, for the ghost is as the man;
And care not thou for dreams from him, but rise —
I hear the steps of Modred in the west,
And with him many of thy people, and knights   60

Once thine, whom thou hast loved, but grosser grown
Than heathen, spitting at their vows and thee.
Right well in heart they know thee for the King.
Arise, go forth and conquer as of old.'

Then spake King Arthur to Sir Bedivere: 65
'Far other is this battle in the west
Whereto we move, than when we strove in youth,
And brake the petty kings, and fought with Rome,
Or thrust the heathen from the Roman wall,
And shook him thro' the north.   Ill doom is mine   70
To war against my people and my knights.
The king who fights his people fights himself.
And they my knights, who loved me once, the stroke
That strikes them dead is as my death to me.
Yet let us hence, and find or feel a way   75
Thro' this blind haze, which ever since I saw
One lying in the dust at Almesbury,
Hath folded in the passes of the world.'

Then rose the King and moved his host by night,
And ever push'd Sir Modred, league by league,   80
Back to the sunset bound of Lyonnesse —
A land of old upheaven from the abyss
By fire, to sink into the abyss again;
Where fragments of forgotten peoples dwelt,
And the long mountains ended in a coast   85
Of ever-shifting sand, and far away
The phantom circle of a moaning sea.
There the pursuer could pursue no more,
And he that fled no further fly the King;
There, that day when the great light of heaven   90
Burn'd at his lowest in the rolling year,

On the waste sand by the waste sea they closed.
Nor ever yet had Arthur fought a fight
Like this last, dim, weird battle of the west.
A deathwhite mist slept over sand and sea: 90
Whereof the chill, to him who breathed it, drew
Down with his blood, till all his heart was cold
With formless fear; and ev'n on Arthur fell
Confusion, since he saw not whom he fought.
For friend and foe were shadows in the mist,   100
And friend slew friend not knowing whom he slew;
And some had visions out of golden youth,
And some beheld the faces of old ghosts
Look in upon the battle; and in the mist
Was many a noble deed, many a base,   105
And chance and craft and strength in single fights,
And ever and anon with host to host
Shocks, and the splintering spear, the hard mail hewn,
Shield-breakings, and the clash of brands, the crash
Of battleaxes on shatter'd helms, and shrieks   110
After the Christ, of those who falling down
Look'd up for heaven, and only saw the mist;
And shouts of heathen and the traitor knights,
Oaths, insult, filth, and monstrous blasphemies,
Sweat, writhing, anguish, laboring of the lungs   1 ?
In that close mist, and cryings for the light,
Moans of the dying, and voices of the dead.

     Last, as by some one deathbed after wail
Of suffering, silence follows, or thro' death
Or deathlike swoon, thus over all that shore,   120
Save for some whisper of the seething seas,
A dead hush fell; but when the dolorous day
Grew drearier toward twilight falling, came

A bitter wind, clear from the North, and blew
The mist aside, and with that wind the tide   125
Rose, and the pale King glanced across the field
Of battle: but no man was moving there;
Nor any cry of Christian heard thereon,
Nor yet of heathen; only the wan wave
Brake in among dead faces, to and fro   130
Swaying the helpless hands, and up and down
Tumbling the hollow helmets of the fallen,
And shiver'd brands that once had fought with Rome,
And rolling far along the gloomy shores
The voice of days of old and days to be.   135

   Then spake King Arthur to Sir Bedivere,
And whiter than the mist that all day long
Had held the field of battle was the King:

   'Hearest thou this great voice that shakes the world,
And wastes the narrow realm whereon we move,   140
And beats upon the faces of the dead,
My dead, as tho' they had not died for me? —
O Bedivere, for on my heart hath fall'n
Confusion, till I know not what I am,
Nor whence I am, nor whether I be King.   145
Behold, I seem but King among the dead.'

   Then spake the bold Sir Bedivere: 'My King,
King everywhere! and so the dead have kings,
There also will I worship thee as King.
Yet still thy life is whole, and still I live   150
Who love thee; but who hates thee, he that brought
The heathen back among us, yonder stands,
Modred, unharm'd, the traitor of thine house

Then spake the King: 'My house hath been my doom.
But call not thou this traitor of my house   155
Who hath but dwelt beneath one roof with me.
My house are rather they who sware my vows,
Yea, even while they brake them, own'd me King.
And well for thee, saying in my dark hour,
When all the purport of my throne hath fail'd,   160
That quick or dead thou holdest me for King.
King am I, whatsoever be their cry;
And one last act of kinghood shalt thou see
Yet, ere I pass.'   And uttering this the King
Made at the man: then Modred smote his liege   165
Hard on that helm which many a heathen sword
Had beaten thin; while Arthur at one blow,
Striking the last stroke with Excalibur,
Slew him, and all but slain himself, he fell.

So all day long the noise of battle roll'd   170
Among the mountains by the winter sea;
Until King Arthur's Table, man by man,
Had fall'n in Lyonnesse about their lord,
King Arthur.   Then, because his wound was deep,
The bold Sir Bedivere uplifted him,   175
And bore him to a chapel nigh the field,
A broken chancel with a broken cross,
That stood on a dark strait of barren land;
On one side lay the Ocean, and on one
Lay a great water, and the moon was full.   180

Then spake King Arthur to Sir Bedivere:
'The sequel of to-day unsolders all
The goodliest fellowship of famous knights
Whereof this world holds record. Such a sleep

They sleep — the men I loved.   I think that we   185
Shall never more, at any future time,
Delight our souls with talk of knightly deeds,
Walking about the gardens and the halls
Of Camelot, as in the days that were.
I perish by this people which I made, —   190
Tho' Merlin sware that I should come again
To rule once more; but, let what will be, be,
I am so deeply smitten thro' the helm
That without help I cannot last till morn.
Thou therefore take my brand Excalibur,   195
Which was my pride: for thou rememberest how
In those old days, one summer noon, an arm
Rose up from out the bosom of the lake,
Clothed in white samite, mystic, wonderful,
Holding the sword — and how I row'd across   200
And took it, and have worn it, like a king;
And, wheresoever I am sung or told
In aftertime, this also shall be known:
But now delay not: take Excalibur,
And fling him far into the middle mere: 205
Watch what thou seest, and lightly bring me word.'

   To him replied the bold Sir Bedivere:
'It is not meet, Sir King, to leave thee thus,
Aidless, alone, and smitten thro' the helm —
A little thing may harm a wounded man;   210
Yet I thy hest will all perform at full,
Watch what I see, and lightly bring thee word.'

   So saying, from the ruin'd shrine he stepp'd,
And in the moon athwart the place of tombs,
Where lay the mighty bones of ancient men,   215

Old knights, and over them the sea-wind sang
Shrill, chill, with flakes of foam.   He, stepping down
By zigzag paths, and juts of pointed rock,
Came on the shining levels of the lake.

There drew he forth the brand Excalibur,   220
And o'er him, drawing it, the winter moon,
Brightening the skirts of a long cloud, ran forth
And sparkled keen with frost against the hilt:
For all the haft twinkled with diamond sparks,
Myriads of topaz-lights, and jacinth-work   225
Of subtlest jewellery.   He gazed so long
That both his eyes were dazzled as he stood,
This way and that dividing the swift mind,
In act to throw: but at the last it seem'd
Better to leave Excalibur conceal'd   230
There in the many-knotted waterflags,
That whistled stiff and dry about the marge.
So strode he back slow to the wounded King.

Then spake King Arthur to Sir Bedivere:
'Hast thou perform'd my mission which I gave?   235
What is it thou hast seen? or what hast heard?'

And answer made the bold Sir Bedivere:
'I heard the ripple washing in the reeds,
And the wild water lapping on the crag.'

To whom replied King Arthur, faint and pale: 240
'Thou hast betray'd thy nature and thy name,
Not rendering true answer, as beseem'd
Thy fealty, nor like a noble knight:
For surer sign had follow'd, either hand,

Or voice, or else a motion of the mere.   245
This is a shameful thing for men to lie.
Yet now, I charge thee, quickly go again,
As thou art lief and dear, and do the thing
I bade thee, watch, and lightly bring me word.'

    Then went Sir Bedivere the second time   250
Across the ridge, and paced beside the mere,
Counting the dewy pebbles, fix'd in thought;
But when he saw the wonder of the hilt,
How curiously and strangely chased, he smote
His palms together, and he cried aloud: 255

    ' And if indeed I cast the brand away,
Surely a precious thing, one worthy note,
Should thus be lost for ever from the earth,
Which might have pleased the eyes of many men.
What good should follow this, if this were done?   260
What harm, undone?   Deep harm to disobey,
Seeing obedience is the bond of rule.
Were it well to obey then, if a king demand
An act unprofitable, against himself?
The King is sick, and knows not what he does.   265
What record, or what relic of my lord
Should be to aftertime, but empty breath
And rumors of a doubt?   But were this kept,
Stored in some treasure-house of mighty kings,
Some one might show it at a joust of arms,   270
Saying, "King Arthur's sword, Excalibur,
Wrought by the lonely maiden of the Lake.
Nine years she wrought it, sitting in the deeps
Upon the hidden bases of the hills."
So might some old man speak in the aftertime   275

To all the people, winning reverence.
But now much honor and much fame were lost.'

So spake he, clouded with his own conceit,
And hid Excalibur the second time,
And so strode back slow to the wounded King.   280

Then spoke King Arthur, breathing heavily:
'What is it thou hast seen? or what hast heard?'

And answer made the bold Sir Bedivere:
'I heard the water lapping on the crag,
And the long ripple washing in the reeds."   285

To whom replied King Arthur, much in wrath:
'Ah, miserable and unkind, untrue,
Unknightly, traitor-hearted! Woe is me!
Authority forgets a dying king,
Laid widow'd of the power in his eye   290
That bow'd the will. I see thee what thou art,
For thou, the latest-left of all my knights,
In whom should meet the offices of all,
Thou wouldst betray me for the precious hilt;
Either from lust of gold, or like a girl   295
Valuing the giddy pleasure of the eyes.
Yet, for a man may fail in duty twice,
And the third time may prosper, get thee hence:
But, if thou spare to fling Excalibur,
I will arise and slay thee with my hands.'   300

Then quickly rose Sir Bedivere, and ran,
And, leaping down the ridges lightly, plunged
Among the bulrush beds, and clutch'd the sword,
And strongly wheel'd and threw it. The great brand

Made lightnings in the splendor of the moon,   305
And flashing round and round, and whirl'd in an arch,
Shot like a streamer of the northern morn,
Seen where the moving isles of winter shock
By night, with noises of the Northern Sea.
So flash'd and fell the brand Excalibur: 310
But ere he dipp'd the surface, rose an arm
Clothed in white samite, mystic, wonderful,
And caught him by the hilt, and brandish'd him
Three times, and drew him under in the mere.
And lightly went the other to the King.   315

Then spoke King Arthur, drawing thicker breath:
'Now see I by thine eyes that this is done.
Speak out: what is it thou hast heard, or seen?'

And answer made the bold Sir Bedivere:
'Sir King, I closed mine eyelids, lest the gems   320
Should blind my purpose, for I never saw,
Nor shall see, here or elsewhere, till I die,
Not tho' I live three lives of mortal men,
So great a miracle as yonder hilt.
Then with both hands I flung him, wheeling him;   325
But when I look'd again, behold an arm,
Clothed in white samite, mystic, wonderful,
That caught him by the hilt, and brandish'd him
Three times, and drew him under in the mere.'

And answer made King Arthur, breathing hard: 330
'My end draws nigh; 'tis time that I were gone.
Make broad thy shoulders to receive my weight,
And bear me to the margin; yet I fear
My wound hath taken cold, and I shall die.'

So saying, from the pavement he half rose,   335
Slowly, with pain, reclining on his arm,
And looking wistfully with wide blue eyes
As in a picture.   Him Sir Bedivere
Remorsefully regarded thro' his tears,
And would have spoken, but he found not words;   340
Then took with care, and kneeling on one knee,
O'er both his shoulders drew the languid hands,
And rising bore him thro' the place of tombs.

But, as he walk'd, King Arthur panted hard,
Like one that feels a nightmare on his bed   345
When all the house is mute.   So sigh'd the King,
Muttering and murmuring at his ear, 'Quick, quick!
I fear it is too late, and I shall die.'
But the other swiftly strode from ridge to ridge,
Clothed with his breath, and looking, as he walk'd,   350
Larger than human on the frozen hills.
He heard the deep behind him, and a cry
Before.   His own thought drove him like a goad.
Dry clash'd his harness in the icy caves
And barren chasms, and all to left and right   355
The bare black cliff clang'd round him, as he based
His feet on juts of slippery crag that rang
Sharp-smitten with the dint of armed heels —
And on a sudden, lo! the level lake,
And the long glories of the winter moon.   360

Then saw they how there hove a dusky barge,
Dark as a funeral scarf from stem to stern,
Beneath them; and descending they were ware
That all the decks were dense with stately forms,
Black-stoled, black-hooded, like a dream — by these   365

Three Queens with crowns of gold: and from them rose
A cry that shiver'd to the tingling stars,
And, as it were one voice, an agony
Of lamentation, like a wind that shrills
All night in a waste land, where no one comes,   370
Or hath come, since the making of the world.

Then murmur'd Arthur, 'Place me in the barge.'
So to the barge they came.   There those three Queens
Put forth their hands, and took the King, and wept.
But she, that rose the tallest of them all   375
And fairest, laid his head upon her lap,
And loosed the shatter'd casque, and chafed his hands,
And call'd him by his name, complaining loud,
And dropping bitter tears against a brow
Striped with dark blood: for all his face was white   380
And colorless, and like the wither'd moon
Smote by the fresh beam of the springing east,
And all his greaves and cuisses dash'd with drops
Of onset; and the light and lustrous curls —
That made his forehead like a rising sun   385
High from the dais-throne — were parch'd with dust;
Or, clotted into points and hanging loose,
Mix'd with the knightly growth that fringed his lips.
So like a shatter'd column lay the King;
Not like that Arthur who, with lance in rest,   390
From spur to plume a star of tournament,
Shot thro' the lists at Camelot, and charged
Before the eyes of ladies and of kings.

Then loudly cried the bold Sir Bedivere:
'Ah! my Lord Arthur, whither shall I go?   395
Where shall I hide my forehead and my eyes?

For now I see the true old times are dead,
When every morning brought a noble chance,
And every chance brought out a noble knight.
Such times have been not since the light that led   400
The holy Elders with the gift of myrrh.
But now the whole Round Table is dissolved
Which was an image of the mighty world,
And I, the last, go forth companionless,
And the days darken round me, and the years,   405
Among new men, strange faces, other minds.'

And slowly answer'd Arthur from the barge:
'The old order changeth, yielding place to new,
And God fulfils himself in many ways,
Lest one good custom should corrupt the world.   410
Comfort thyself: what comfort is in me?
I have lived my life, and that which I have done
May He within himself make pure! but thou,
If thou shouldst never see my face again,
Pray for my soul.   More things are wrought by prayer
Than this world dreams of.   Wherefore, let thy voice   416
Rise like a fountain for me night and day.
For what are men better than sheep or goats
That nourish a blind life within the brain,
If, knowing God, they lift not hands of prayer   420
Both for themselves and those who call them friend?
For so the whole round earth is every way
Bound by gold chains about the feet of God.
But now farewell.   I am going a long way
With these thou seest — if indeed I go   425
(For all my mind is clouded with a doubt) —
To the island-valley of Avilion;
Where falls not hail, or rain, or any snow,

Nor ever wind blows loudly; but it lies
Deep-meadow'd, happy, fair with orchard lawns   430
And bowery hollows crown'd with summer sea,
Where I will heal me of my grievous wound.'

    So said he, and the barge with oar and sail
Moved from the brink, like some full-breasted swan
That, fluting a wild carol ere her death,   435
Ruffles her pure cold plume, and takes the flood
With swarthy webs.   Long stood Sir Bedivere
Revolving many memories, till the hull
Look'd one black dot against the verge of dawn,
And on the mere the wailing died away.   440

    But when that moan had past for evermore,
The stillness of the dead world's winter dawn
Amazed him, and he groaned, 'The King is gone.'
And therewithal came on him the weird rhyme,
'From the great deep to the great deep he goes.'   445

    Whereat he slowly turn'd and slowly clomb
The last hard footstep of that iron crag;
Thence mark'd the black hull moving yet, and cried,
'He passes to be King among the dead,
And after healing of his grievous wound   450
He comes again; but — if he comes no more —
O me, be yon dark Queens in yon black boat,
Who shriek'd and wail'd, the three whereat we gazed
On that high day, when, clothed with living light,
They stood before his throne in silence, friends   455
Of Arthur, who should help him at his need?'

    Then from the dawn it seem'd there came, but faint
As from beyond the limit of the world,

Like the last echo born of a great cry,
Sounds, as if some fair city were one voice   460
Around a king returning from his wars.

Thereat once more he moved about, and clomb
Even to the highest he could climb, and saw,
Straining his eyes beneath an arch of hand,
Or thought he saw, the speck that bare the King,   465
Down that long water opening on the deep
Somewhere far off, pass on and on, and go
From less to less and vanish into light.
And the new sun rose bringing the new year.

THE OATH OF KNIGHTHOOD FROM
GUINEVERE

To reverence the King, as if he were
Their conscience, and their conscience as their King,
To break the heathen and uphold the Christ,
To ride abroad redressing human wrongs,
To speak no slander, no, nor listen to it,
To honor his own word as if his God's,
To lead sweet lives in purest chastity,
To love one maiden only, cleave to her,
And worship her by years of noble deeds,
Until they won her.

NOTES.

THE COMING OF ARTHUR.

THIS Idyll was not first, but at least sixth, in actual order of composition. Tennyson plainly made use of it to assemble some loose threads of the Arthurian fabric, which he had now pretty well completed in his mind. His version of the narrative is, as has been suggested in the Introduction to this edition, very different from that of Malory. It is less simple, straightforward, and mediæval, more mystical, ideal, and modern. It omits important incidents given in *Le Morte Darthur*, and introduces altogether new ones. For instance, it makes Arthur's marriage of far greater account to Arthur's spiritual life than does Malory, and of less account to his career; for, according to the old narrative, the Round Table itself and many of the knights came as Guinevere's dower. Tennyson also frequently changes the order of events as given by Malory.

Here is the substance of Malory's account of Arthur's marriage (Book I, chaps. xvii and xviii, and Book III, chaps. i, ii, and v): —

"Then there came word that the King Rience of North Wales made great war on King Leodegrance of Cameliard, for the which thing Arthur was wroth, for he loved him well, and hated King Rience, for he was always against him. . . . And then King Arthur, and King Ban, and King Bors departed with their fellowship, a twenty thousand, and came within six days into the country of Cameliard, and there rescued King Leodegrance, and slew there much people of King Rience, unto the number of ten thousand men, and put them to flight. And then had these three kings great cheer of King Leodegrance, that thanked them of their great goodness, that they could revenge him of his enemies; and there had Arthur the first sight of Guenever, the king's daughter of Cameliard, and ever after he loved her. After they were wedded, as it telleth in the book."

It was some time later, by Malory's account, that the wedding took place. The rest of the first Book and all of the second are occupied with adventures of various sorts. Then, at the beginning of Book III: —

"In the beginning of Arthur, after he was chosen king by adventure and by grace; for the most part of the barons knew not that he was Uther Pendragon's son, but as Merlin made it openly known. But yet many kings and lords held great war against him for that cause, but well Arthur overcame them all, for the most part the days of his life he was ruled much by the counsel of Merlin. So it fell on a time King Arthur said unto Merlin, My barons will let me have no rest, but needs I must take a wife, and I will now take but by thy counsel and thine advice. It is well done, said Merlin, that ye take a wife, for a man of your bounty and noblesse should not be without a wife. Now is there any that ye love more than another? Yea, said King Arthur, I love Guenever the king's daughter, Leodegrance of the land of Cameliard, the which holdeth in his house the Table Round that ye told he had of my father Uther. And this damosel is the most valiant and fairest lady that I know living, or yet that ever I could find. Sir, said Merlin, as of her beauty and fairness she is one of the fairest alive, but, an ye loved her not so well as ye do, I should find you a damosel of beauty and of goodness that should like you and please you, an your heart were not set; but then as a man's heart is set, he will be loath to return. That is truth, said King Arthur. But Merlin warned the king covertly that Guenever was not wholesome for him to take to wife, for he warned him that Lancelot should love her, and she him again; and so he turned his tale to the adventures of Sangreal. Then Merlin desired of the king for to have men with him that should enquire of Guenever, and so the king granted him, and Merlin went forth unto King Leodegrance of Cameliard, and told him of the desire of the king that he would have unto his wife Guenever his daughter. That is to me, said King Leodegrance, the best tidings that ever I heard, that so worthy a king of prowess and noblesse will wed my daughter. And as for my lands, I will give him, wist I it might please him, but he hath lands enow, him needeth none, but I shall send him a gift shall please him much more, for I shall give him the Table Round, the which Uther Pendragon gave me, and when it is full complete.

then is an hundred knights and fifty. And as for an hundred good knights I have myself, but I faute fifty, for so many have been slain in my days. And so Leodegrance delivered his daughter Guenever unto Merlin, and the Table Round with the hundred knights, and so they rode freshly, with great royalty, what by water and what by land, till that they came nigh unto London. . . . When King Arthur heard of the coming of Guenever and the hundred knights with the Table Round, then King Arthur made great joy for her coming, and that rich present, and said openly, This fair lady is passing welcome unto me, for I have loved her long, and therefore there is nothing so lief to me. And these knights with the Round Table please me more than great riches. And in all haste the king let ordain for the marriage and the coronation, in the most honorable wise that could be devised. . . . Then was the high feast made ready, and the king was wedded at Camelot unto Dame Guenever in the church of Saint Stephen's, with great solemnity."

The pronunciation of the proper names varies somewhat. In general however, the stress comes early, as Gui'nevere, Ga'wain La'ncelot (a dissyllable).

1. Leodegran. Lord of one of the many tiny realms into which Britain was divided. As with most of the places mentioned in the *Idylls*, nobody knows just where **Cameliard** was. Perhaps in Wales, perhaps in Scotland, perhaps nowhere. Arthur's Britain is a land of legend and romance, and there is not much use in trying to make an accurate map of it.

5. ere Arthur came. Arthur's time is supposed to have been about 500 A.D. Something like a century earlier, the last Roman legions had left England. In 410, Emperor Honorius formally freed Britain from allegiance to Rome. But this left southern Britain at the mercy of the wild Picts and Scots of the North. About the middle of the fifth century, the Britons sent a desperate appeal to Rome to send her legions back for their defence: " The barbarians drive us ―to the sea," they cried; " the sea throws us back on the barbarians; thus two modes of death await us, we are either slain or drowned." Rome came to the rescue — for the last time; and shortly afterward, according to Littledale, the Saxons were called in to hold the Northern tribes in check, and so a new source of discord entered England.

8. the heathen host. Apparently the Saxons and Danes; but Tennyson seems to be vague in distinguishing these enemies of the native Britons from the Picts and Scots. See " the heathen horde," line 36.

13. Aurelius. Aurelius Emrys, according to Green (*Making of England*), was " a descendant of the last Roman general who claimed the purple as an Emperor in Britain." As **King Uther** was Aurelius's brother as well as successor, King Arthur belonged to this same Roman line; though Tennyson prefers to hint at some less earthly origin for his hero.

29. human sucklings. There are said to be authentic cases of children reared by wolves; at all events it is one of the oldest romantic fables, as for instance in the myth of Romulus and Remus, and in Kipling's tale of *Mowgli*.

38–40. And on the spike, etc. These lines have often been quoted as an example of Tennyson's use of alliteration and assonance.

46. Arthur yet had done no deed. Tennyson chooses to represent Arthur as owing the beginning of his valor and fame in part to his love for Guinevere. But according to Malory, Arthur's fame as a fighting man was safe before he fought for Leodegrance.

50. The golden symbol. The device of the golden dragon which was Uther's symbol and from which the name " Pendragon" was derived. See *Lancelot and Elaine*, line 432.

72. Gorlois. Called by Malory simply the Duke of Tintagil; the first husband of Igraine (Ygerne) the mother of Arthur.

73. Anton. Called by Malory Sir Ector. His wife nursed Arthur in infancy.

94–133. This whole passage was added in the second edition. It introduces the idea of some mystical power protecting Arthur (lines 105–108), and also the idea of his love for, and trust in, Sir Lancelot (lines 124–131).

103. battle. Line of battle.

134. the foughten field. So Shakespeare, *Henry VIII*, iv. 6, 18 : " This glorious and well foughten field."

146. Arthur's birth. As we have seen from the passage quoted above, Malory's King Leodegrance makes no question of Arthur's birth. The story of his birth takes up the two opening chapters of *Le Morte Darthur*. In this story, at once, **Merlin** is involved. To King Uther as to King Arthur, Merlin, according to the old story, played the part not only of magician, but of adviser and practical helper in various matters. Throughout the *Idylls* he appears as a more mystical figure, though he is credited with the building of Camelot by magic means.

152. Merlin's master (so they call him) Bleys. "They" in the parenthesis probably means Malory, who tells about Merlin's reporting one of Arthur's battles to a "Bleise," and of Bleise's writing it down: "All the battles that were done in Arthur's days Merlin did his master Bleise do write." Those who discover a complete allegory of life in the *Idylls* interpret Merlin as "intellect in the service of spiritual ideals."

208. that same night, etc. According to Malory, Arthur was about two years old when King Uther on his deathbed proclaimed him his heir. It was not generally known, though; and on attaining manhood as the supposed son of Sir Ector (called by Tennyson Anton), he first proved his true birth by the test of drawing the sword from the stone. It is strange that Tennyson made no use of this romantic test in his version of the story. (See *Le Morte Darthur*, Book I, chaps. v, vi.)

243. In Malory's account, **Modred**, or Mordred, becomes the instrument of Fate, to Arthur's undoing. **Bellicent** was his mother, and the half-sister of Arthur.

275. three fair queens. Said by Henry van Dyke and others to represent Faith, Hope, and Charity. But as with other mystical figures in the *Idylls*, it is doubtful whether we can press any interpretation of them too closely.

282. the Lady of the Lake. Supposed to symbolize the Church, or religion.

284. samite. A silk of heavy and rich texture.

295. Excalibur. In Malory it is considerably later that Arthur gets Excalibur. Arthur's sword has been broken in a fight with King Pellinore:

"And as they rode, Arthur said, I have no sword. No force,

162 THE COMING OF ARTHUR.

said Merlin, hereby is a sword that shall be yours, an I may. So they rode till they came to a lake, the which was a fair water and broad, and in the midst of the lake Arthur was ware of an arm clothed in white samite, that held a fair sword in that hand. Lo! said Merlin, yonder is that sword that I spake of. With that they saw a damosel going upon the lake. What damosel is that? said Arthur. That is the Lady of the Lake, said Merlin."

Arthur asks the Lady of the Lake for the sword, and she gives it on condition that he will do her a favor at need. "Excalibur" means "cut-steel." According to Malory, the magical properties belonged to the scabbard rather than to the sword itself.

298. elfin Urim. Fairy jewels. The breastplate, or Urim, of the Jewish high-priest (see *Exodus*, xxviii, 30) was ornamented with gems.

362. fairy changeling. Alluding to the old belief that fairies sometimes exchanged their own for human children.

401. riddling triplets of old time. The three-line jingles in which the Celtic bards often cast their songs and prophecies.

421. again to come. It was long a tradition in Britain that Arthur was not dead, but would return to a more glorious rule over a better world. At the end of his tale (Book XXI, chap. vii) Malory says: "Yet some men say in many parts of England that King Artur is not dead, but had by the will of our Lord Jesu into another place; and men say that he shall come again, and he shall win the holy cross. I will not say it shall be so, but rather I will say: here in this world he changed his life. But many men say that there is written upon his tomb this verse: Hic jacet Arthurus Rex, quondam Rex que futurus (Here lies King Arthur, King that has been and King to be)."

481–501. Blow trumpet, etc. "A piece of glorious literature," says Stopford Brooke. "It embodies the thought of the poem, grips the whole meaning of it together. And its sound is the sound of martial triumph, of victorious weapons in battle, and of knights in arms. We hear in the carefully varied chorus, in the very rattle and shattering of the vowels in the words, the beating of axe upon helm, and shield on shield. Rugged, clanging, clashing lines, — it is a splendid effort of art."

504. The slowly-fading mistress of the world. See Note, line 5 above.

505. But Arthur spake, etc. All this about Arthur and Rome is without historic truth. Says Littledale: " In the curt answer to the Roman envoys, and the words ' Arthur strove with Rome,' the poet in a few lines disposes of an amount of pseudo-history that occupies nearly half of Geoffrey's [Geoffrey of Monmouth's] entire narrative. But even Tennyson's brief allusion to Arthur's Roman war has no foundation in history."

517. twelve great battles. See *Lancelot and Elaine,* 286–303.

GARETH AND LYNETTE.

After some four hundred lines of introduction, which are his own in idea as well as form, Tennyson follows Malory closely in this *Idyll.* The story makes up one of the longest episodes in *Le Morte Darthur,* occupying the whole of Book VII.

1. Lot and Bellicent. King and Queen of Orkney. Bellicent was the mother of Modred, or Mordred, who is the villain of the Arthurian legend. Gawain, already a knight of the Round Table, was another son. In Malory's version **Gareth,** who goes by the nickname "Beaumains," does not actually serve in the kitchen, but remains a pensioner for a year and a day.

3. spate. Torrent or freshet. A Scotch word often used by the poet Burns.

18. Heaven yield her for it. Old English " yielden," to pay, to reward. Shakespeare several times uses the word in this sense.

27. proven. Tested.

28. Modred for want of worthier. Neither of Modred's brothers has any respect for him, — the " yellow " member of the family.

46. Book of Hours. An illuminated missal, or prayer-book.

51. a leash of kings. Hounds were held in groups on the leash, or cord, till loosed upon the prey. Hence a leash came to mean three or more of anything.

59. true love . . . had risked himself. Would have risked itself.

64. Had ventured — had the thing been. Would have ventured if the thing had been.

70. Gareth shifts suddenly from his parable to its application in his own case.

87. often chance. Often here means "frequent." Bellicent says, in effect, " The kind of thing that so often happens in the rough encounters of the tourney, frightens me."

90. burns. Brooks.

94–95. to grace Thy climbing life, etc. To give beauty to your youth, and comfort to my age.

104. But. Only.

122. frequent. The old sense of " familiar."

133. Not proven. Gareth scornfully echoes his mother's phrase (line 127).

139. one: unwaveringly one. Unshakably steadfast, consistent.

145. An Elizabethan play or pun on the two meanings of " quick. "

151. kitchen-knaves. Knave meant " boy," then " servant." Compare German "Knabe," " boy."

157. villain. Villainous, or slavish: compare " villein," serf.

160. closed. Shut in, protected.

162. thrall. An Anglo-Saxon word: servant or serf.

172. outward purpose. Purpose to go outward, to escape from home.

176. still. In the older sense of continually, always. So used habitually in Elizabethan English.

185. Camelot. A prose sketch was found among Tennyson's papers which gave this description of Arthur's capital city: " On the latest limit of the West, in the land of Lyonesse, where save the rocky isles of Scilly all is now wild sea, rose the sacred mount of Camelot. It rose from the deeps, with gardens and bowers and palaces, and at the top of the mount was King Arthur's hall and the holy minster with the cross of gold."

191. Prick'd. Pierced.

193. Anon. Presently.

202. glamour. Enchantment.

212. the Lady of the Lake. This description of Tennyson's Lady of the Lake (very different from the lady of Malory) most clearly suggests her as a personification of Religion.

218. either worn. Each battered and tarnished.

225. those three Queens. See *The Coming of Arthur*, line 275, and Note.

229. dragon-boughts. Dragon coils, or folds.

258. built to music. Like Troy and Thebes, and Milton's Pandemonium. See *Paradise Lost*, I, 110.

280. the Riddling of the Bards. See *The Coming of Arthur*, line 401, and Note.

293. she. Gareth's mother, Bellicent.

298. did their days. Recorded, or engraved. So we speak of " doing " embroidery.

314. doom. Judgment, not necessarily adverse.

315. in fear to find Gawain or Modred. His brothers, Knights of Arthur's court, who would recognize him and spoil his game.

321–325. As we see later, this praise of Arthur's knights is not altogether justified in the long run.

327. reft. Past form of " reave " (see line 411); to take away, as here, or to deprive, as in line 331.

351. standeth seized of. Remains in possession of: a term still used in law.

355. wreak. Avenge.

359. seneschal. Steward.

367. Aurelius Emrys. See *The Coming of Arthur*, line 13, and Note.

369. Lest that rough humor. In Malory's narrative, King Arthur is a very human person. This is one of the relatively few passages in Tennyson's story that give such an impression of him.

380. charlock. Wild mustard.

398. blazon'd. On these shields, which belonged to the knights who were altogether " proven," the engraved arms or device was also decorated in the proper heraldic colors.

422. cloth of lead. That is, in a coffin.

427. nor lets. Without letting.

431. Last, Gareth leaning both hands heavily, etc. This is the point at which Malory's story of Gareth begins: —

" Right so came into the hall two men well beseen and richly, and upon their shoulders there leaned the goodliest young man and the fairest that ever they all saw, and he was large and long and broad in the shoulders, and well visaged, and the fairest and the largest handed that ever man saw, but he fared as though he might not go nor bear himself but he leaned upon their shoulders. . . . Then this much young man pulled himself aback, and easily stretched up straight, saying, King Arthur, God you bless and all your fair fellowship, and in especial the fellowship of the Table Round. And for this cause I am come hither, to pray you and require you to give me three gifts, and they shall not be unreasonably asked, but that ye may worshipfully and honourably grant them me, and to you no great hurt nor loss. And the first done and gift I will ask now, and the other two gifts I will ask this day twelvemonth, wheresomever ye hold your high feast. Now ask, said Arthur, and ye shall have your asking. Now, sir, this is my petition for this feast, that ye will give me meat and drink sufficiently for this twelvemonth, and at that day I will ask mine other two gifts. My fair son, said Arthur, ask better, for this is but a simple asking; for my heart giveth me to thee greatly, that thou art come of men of worship, and greatly my conceit faileth me but thou shalt prove a man of right great worship. Sir, said he, thereof be as it may be, I have asked that I will ask. Well, said the king, ye shall have meat and drink enough; I never defended that none, neither my friend nor my foe. But what is thy name I would wit? I cannot tell you, said he. That is marvel, said the king, that thou knowest not thy name, and thou art the goodliest young man one that ever I saw. Then the king betook him to Sir Kay the steward, and charged him that he should give him of all manner of meats and drinks of the best, and also that he had no manner of finding as though he were a lord's son. That shall little need, said Sir Kay, to do such cost upon him; for I dare undertake he is a villain born, and never will make man, for an he had come of gentlemen he would have asked of you horse and armor, but such as he is, such he asketh. And sithen he hath no name, I shall give him a name that shall be Beaumains, that is Fair-hands, and into the kitchen I shall bring him, and there he shall have fat brose every day, that he shall be as fat by the twelvemonth's end as a pork hog. Right so the two men departed and beleft him to Sir 'Kay, that scorned him and mocked him." Malory, Book VII, chap. i.

441. so thou wilt no goodlier. Since you ask for nothing better.

447. brewis. Broth.

454. fluent. Flowing.

465. Fine-face, Fair-hands. In Malory Gareth is known as Beaumains (Fair-hands) during the time of his probation.

476. broach. Spit, on which meat was cooked over the open fire.

490. Caer-Eryri's highest. The summit of Snowdon, a Welsh mountain, the highest in England or Wales.

492. the Isle Avilion. Perhaps at Glastonbury. "But in Arthurian romance," says Macaulay, "it is a kind of mythical 'isle of the Blest,' situated somewhere in the ocean." See *The Passing of Arthur*, 427.

507–509. So there were any trial of mastery, etc. "And when there were any masteries done," says Malory, "thereat would he be, and there might none cast bar or stone to him by two yards."

528. from Satan's foot to Peter's knee. From Hell to Heaven.

573–649. In Malory's narrative there is no preliminary interview between Arthur and Gareth before the coming of Lynette:—

"So it passed on till the feast of Whitsuntide, and at that time the king held it at Carlion in the royallest wise, like as he did yearly. But the king would no meat eat upon the Whitsunday, until he heared some adventures. Then came there a squire to the king, and said, Sir, ye may go to your meat, for here cometh a damosel with some strange adventures. Then the king was glad and sat him down. Right so there came the damosel into the hall, and saluted the king, and prayed him of succor "(Book VII, chap. ii). The " damosel " then tells him what the adventure is to be, and asks for a champion, though she does not speak of Sir Lancelot. "With these words came before the king Beaumains [Gareth] while the damosel was there, and thus he said: Sir King, God thank you I have been this twelvemonth in your kitchen, and have had your full sustenance, and now I will ask my two gifts that be behind. Ask, upon my peril, said the king. Sir, this shall be my two gifts, first that you will grant me to have this adventure of the damosel, for it belongeth unto me. Thou shalt have it, said the king, I grant

it thee. Then, sir, this is the other gift, that ye shall bid Sir Launcelot du Lake to make me knight, for of him will I be made knight
and else of none. And when I am passed, I pray you let him ride
after me, and make me knight when I require him. All this shall
be done, said the king. Fie on thee, said the damosel, shall I have
none but one that is your kitchen page? Then was she wroth and
took her horse and departed." Malory, Book VII, chaps. ii, iii.

584. lonest hold. Most solitary castle or stronghold.

586. that best blood. The sacramental wine, the blood of
Christ.

607. or a holy life. Or she will become a nun.

615. from the moment. According to impulse.

642. Slew the may-white. See "May-blossom" line 575.
"The may," in England, means the white hawthorn, or white-thorn,
a favorite symbol of spring and purity.

647. the slope street. Slanting. So Milton in *Comus*, line
98: "the slope sun."

662–674. According to Malory, a dwarf appears with the horse
and trappings: "thereat had all the court much marvel from whence
came all that gear."

686–692. but as the cur, etc. A simile in the Homeric fashion
— an idyll or "little picture" in itself. There is something of the
kind just above in lines 670–674.

690-718. "Then Sir Kay," says Malory, "said all open in the
hall, I will ride after my boy in the kitchen, to wit whether he will
know me for his better. Said Sir Launcelot and Sir Gawaine, Yet
abide at home. So Sir Kay made him ready, and took his horse
and his spear, and rode after him."

698. his youth. Arthur's youth.

711. For that did never he whereon ye rail. For the person
you are railing against never did that.

712. served the king in thee. Served you as representing
the authority of the King.

721. were Sir Lancelot lack'd. Even if Sir Lancelot were
denied me.

729. agaric in the holt. Mushroom in the wood. Most
poisonous mushrooms are found among trees rather than in the
open.

734–740. for there was Kay, etc. By Malory's account, Sir Kay comes up with Gareth as soon as he has overtaken the "damosel." Kay is overthrown, and Gareth challenges to joust a knight who had stood by watching. They have a long bout, which ends in a draw; the knight declares himself Lancelot, and dubs Gareth knight. Gareth then overtakes Lynette a second time. "When he had overtaken the damosel, anon she said, What dost thou here? . . . Weenest thou, said she, that I allow thee for yonder knight that thou killest? Nay, truly, for thou slewest him unhappily and cowardly; therefore turn again, kitchen page, I know thee well, for Sir Kay named thee Beaumains. What art thou but a luske lout and a turner of broaches and a ladle-washer? Damosel, said Beaumains, say to me what you will, I will not go from you whatsomever ye say, for I have undertaken to King Arthur for to achieve your adventure, and so shall I finish it to the end; either I shall die therefore. . . . I shall assay, said Beaumains."

739. shock'd. Came together violently.

749. unhappiness. Tennyson follows Malory's diction in using "unhappiness" and "mishappiness" with the meaning of mischance, bad luck.

778. mere. A still pool or lake.

796. oilily bubbled up. A good example of Tennyson's skill in making sound echo meaning.

808. guerdon. Reward.

832–851. "Fie, fie, said she, Sir Knight, ye are uncourteous to set a kitchen page afore me; him beseemeth better to stick a swine than to sit afore a damosel of high parage. Then the knight was ashamed at her words, and took him up, and set him at a side board, and set himself afore him, and so all that night they had good cheer and merry rest."

908. Avanturine. A kind of quartz spangled with mica.

935. avoid. The old meaning of "depart."

943. drew. Drew his sword.

951. grace. Favor.

996. worship. Honor.

1008. marches. Borders.

1052. mavis, merle. Thrush, blackbird.

1102. ill uses. Evil habits.

1132–1153. In Malory's narrative, the damosel's repentance **is** less romantic, though complete:

"O Jesu, marvel have I, said the damosel, what manner a man ye be, for it may never be otherwise but that ye be come of noble blood, for so foul nor shamefully did never woman rule a knight as I have done you, and ever courteously ye have suffered me, and that came never but of a gentle blood. . . . Alas, she said, fair Beaumains, forgive me all that I have missaid or done against thee. With all my heart, said he, I forgive it you, for you did nothing but as ye should do, for all your words pleased me; and damosel, said Beaumains, sine it liketh you to say thus fair unto me, wit ye well it gladdeth my heart greatly, and now meseemeth there is no knight living but I am able enough for him.

1163. comb. Usually spelled "combe": a hollow.

1172. In letters like to those the vexillary, etc. "Referring to the Latin inscription carved by the vexillary, or standard-bearer, of the second (Roman) legion upon a cliff overhanging the little river Gelt near Brampton in Cumberland (England)." Rolfe.

1184. error. In the literal sense, "wandering."

1185–1189. As has been shown, Malory places the meeting of Gareth and Lancelot at the beginning of the adventure. Thereafter follow the combats with the three brothers, — the Black Knight, the Green Knight, and the Red Knight: Phosphorus (Morning Star), Meridies, (Noon), and Nox (Night) of line 1174 above.

1281. Arthur's harp. Probably the star Arcturus. Mentioned later in *The Last Tournament*, lines 331–336: —

> " . . . Dost thou know the star
> We call the harp of Arthur up in heaven? "

1373–1385. This incident has no place in the older **versions** of the Arthurian tale.

1392. he that told the tale. That is, Malory, who makes a long story of it after the point where Tennyson stops. In it, Gareth, before he finally gains the hand of "the lady Lioness," wins an open tournament in which most of the knights of the Round Table take part. Lynette (or Linet) turns out to be something of an enchantress, and not at all in love with Gareth. She marries one of the other knights, Sir Gaderis.

LANCELOT AND ELAINE.

2. Astolat. Malory says Astolat was at Guilford (Surrey), but Tennyson places it somewhere on the Thames.

Tennyson takes his main story here almost directly from Malory. But he begins the tale more artfully, with the statement of Elaine's possession of the shield; then follows the account of the manner in which it came into her hands.

22, 23. Caerlyle. Probably in Cumberland; **Caerleon,** in South Wales; and **Camelot** in Cornwall (see note on *Gareth and Lynette,* line 985).

8–12. This passage well illustrates the difference between Tennyson's " poetic diction " and ordinary speech. To substitute simpler diction for words like " soilure," " blazon'd," " tinct," etc., would be to spoil the flavor of the description.

tinct. Color.

31. for the great diamond, etc. According to Malory, it is on another occasion that Arthur offers a diamond for a tourney prize; but it has no such special importance as in this Idyll. The romantic story of Arthur's finding of the diamond is of Tennyson's invention.

35. Lyonnesse. A fabulous tract of land supposed to have extended from Cornwall to the Scilly Islands, and to have been sunk in the sea.

36. tarn. A mountain pool or small lake.

37. clave. Old preterite of " cleave ": in the sense of "clung."

53. shingly scaur. A slanting ledge covered with small stones.

59. Divinely. Providentially.

67. still. In the older meaning of "always."

76. this world's hugest. London.

91. tale. Number. **boon**. Gift.

94. lets me from the saddle. Hinders, keeps me. In modern usage the word retains this meaning only in the game of tennis.

118–119. This is surely a false note from the matchless knight: a vulgar and caddish taunt; but this whole scene is on a low plane of feeling.

149. But knowing. Merely from the knowledge.

158–205. "And so upon the morn early Sir Launcelot heard mass and brake his fast, and so took his leave of the queen and departed. And then he rode so much till he came to Astolat, that is Guildford; and there it happed him in the eventide he came to an old baron's place that hight Sir Bernard of Astolat. . . . So when Sir Launcelot was in his lodging, and unarmed him in his chamber, the old baron and hermit came to him making his reverence, and welcomed him in the best manner; but the old knight knew not Sir Launcelot. Fair sir, said Sir Launcelot to his host, I would pray you to lend me a shield that were not openly known, for mine is well known. Sir, said his host, ye shall have your desire, for meseemeth ye be one of the likeliest knights of the world, and therefore I shall show you friendship. Sir, wit you well I have two sons that were but late made knights, and the eldest hight Sir Tirre, and he was hurt that same day he was made knight, that he may not ride, and his shield ye shall have, for that is not known I dare say but here, and in no place else. And my youngest son hight Lawaine, and if it please you, he shall ride with you unto that jousts; and he is of his age strong and wight." — Malory, Book XVIII, chap. ix.

216. all was jest and joke. See line 175, above.

222. So ye will grace me. If you will honor me.

235. Full courtly, yet not falsely. Very courteously, yet without pretending more interest than he felt.

263. as in a smaller time. Like a modern aristocrat.

269. glanced at Guinevere. Alluded to her in passing.

279. on Baden hill. A hill in Dorsetshire where the Britons defeated the West Saxons in a battle in the year 520.

297. the wild white Horse. A white horse was the emblem of the Saxons.

310–311. nor cares for triumph. Malory represents Arthur as fond of winning in the jousts and quite humanly jealous of Lancelot's superiority.

338. rathe. Early, soon. Compare: "Bring the rathe primrose," Milton's *Lycidas*, 142. "Rather" is the comparative of this now obsolete word.

377. yet-unblazon'd shield. With the pattern or device as yet uncolored, because Torre had not yet won to full knighthood, before his injury.

382. I am your squire. It was among the squire's duties to look after his knight's armor.

440. tender. Delicate.

468–473. " O mercy Jesu, said Sir Gawaine, what knight is that knight yonder that does so marvellous deeds of arms in that field? I wot well what he is, said King Arthur, but as at this time I will not name him. Sir, said Sir Gawaine, I would say it were Sir Launcelot by his riding and his buffets that I see him deal, but ever meseemeth it should not be he for that he beareth the red sleeve upon his head, for I wist him never bear token at no lists of lady nor gentlewoman." — Malory, Book XVIII, chap. xi.

513–516. " And forthwith Sir Lavaine drew the truncheon out of his side, and he gave great shriek and a marvellous grisly groan, and the blood burst out nigh a pint at once, that at the last he sank down, and so swooned pale and deadly. . . . And then with great pain Sir Lavaine halp him upon his horse. And then they rode a great wallop together, and ever Sir Launcelot bled that it ran down to the earth; and so by fortune they came to that hermitage the which was under a wood, and a great cliff on the other side, and a fair water running under it." Malory, Book XVIII, chap. xiii.

540–541. We will do him. The *we* is the " royal plural." **customary.** Commonplace.

555–556. therewithal Sir Modred's brother. That is, Gawain had bad blood in him.

592. fine. Minute, trifling.

634. accorded. Agreed, assented.

653. the hern we slipp'd her at. The heron we loosed her at.

658–709. Comparison with the original passage in Malory shows how completely his idea of Gawain differs from that of Tennyson: " Ah, mercy, said Sir Gawaine, now is my heart more heavier than ever it was tofore. Why? said Elaine. For I have great cause, said Sir Gawaine; is that knight that owneth this shield your love? Yea truly, said she, my love he is, God would I were his love. Truly, said Sir Gawaine, fair damsel, ye have right, for, and he be your love, ye love the most honourable knight of the world, and the man of most worship. So me thought ever, said the damsel, for never, or that time, for no knight that ever I saw loved I never none erst. God grant, said Sir Gawaine, that either of you may rejoice other, but that is in a great adventure. But truly, said Sir Gawaine unto the damsel, ye may say ye have a fair grace, for why, I have known that noble knight this four and twenty year, and never or that day I nor none other knight, I dare make it good, saw nor heard say that ever he bare token or sign of no lady, gentlewoman, nor maiden, at no jousts nor tournament. And therefore fair maiden, said Sir Gawaine, ye are much beholden to him to give him thanks. But I dread me, said Sir Gawaine, that ye shall never see him in this world, and that is great pity that ever was of earthly knight. Alas, said she, how may this be? Is he slain? I say not so, said Sir Gawaine, but wit ye well, he is grievously wounded, by all manner of signs, and by men's sight more likely to be dead then to be on live; and wit ye well he is the noble knight Sir Launcelot, for by this shield I know him. Alas, said the fair maiden of Astolat, how may this be, and what was his hurt? Truly, said Sir Gawaine, the man in the world that loved him best hurt him so, and I dare say, said Sir Gawaine, and that knight that hurt him knew the very certainty that he had hurt Sir Launcelot, it would be the most sorrow that ever came to his heart. Now, fair father, said then Elaine, I require you give me leave to ride and to seek him, or else I wot well I shall go out of my mind, for I shall never stint till that I find him and my brother Sir Lavaine. Do as it liketh you, said her father, for me right sore repenteth of the hurt of that noble knight. Right so the maid made her ready, and before Sir Gawaine making great dole. Then on the morn Sir Gawaine came to king Arthur, and told him how he had found Sir Launcelot's shield in the keeping of the fair maiden of Astolat. All that knew I aforehand, said king Arthur, and that caused me I would not suffer you to have ado at the great jousts: for I espied, said king Arthur, when he came in till his lodging, full late in the evening in Astolat. But marvel have I, said Arthur, that ever he would bear any sign of any damsel: for, or [before] now, I never heard say nor knew that ever he bare any token of none earthly woman. By my head, said Sir Gawaine, the fair maiden of Astolat loveth him marvellously well; what it meaneth I cannot say; and she is ridden after to seek him. So the king and all came to London, and there Sir Gawaine openly disclosed to all the court that it was Sir Launcelot that jousted best." — Malory. Book XVIII, chap. xiv.

728. Marr'd her friend's aim with pale tranquillity. Foiled her friend's purpose by her quiet self-possession.

773. Her suit allow'd. Her request granted.

798. His own far blood. His own distant relatives.

831. blazed. Blazoned, revealed.

870. straiten'd. Bound him closely.

880. grace. Beauty.

923. that I live to hear . . . is yours. The fact that I am alive to listen to you, I owe to you.

929. had I chosen to wed, etc. " For wit ye well, fair maiden, I might have married an I had would, but I never applied me to be married yet." Malory, Book XVIII, chap. xix.

939. quit. Requite.

1092. ghostly man. Priest.

1129. dole. Dolor, mourning — a word of Malory's.

1092. " So when she had thus endured a ten days, that she fretted so that she must needs pass out of this world, then she shrived her clean, and received her Creator." — Malory, Book XVIII, chap. xix.

1109–1122. " And while my body is hot let this letter be put in my right hand; and my hand bound fast with the letter until that I be cold; and let me be put in a fair bed with all the richest clothes that I have about me, and so let my bed and all my richest clothes be laid with me in a chariot unto the next place where Thames is; and there let me be put within a barget, and but one man with me, such as ye trust to steer me thither, and that my barget be covered with black samite over and over; thus father I beseech you let it be done." — Malory, Book XVIII, chap. xix.

1264–1274. " Then the king brake it, and made a clerk to read it, and this was the intent of the letter: Most Noble Knight, Sir Launcelot, now hath death made us two at debate for your love. I was your lover that men called the Fair Maiden of Astolat; there-fore unto all ladies I make my moan, yet pray for my soul, and bury me at least, and offer ye my mass-penny: this is my last request. . . . Pray for my soul, Sir Launcelot, as thou art peerless." — Malory, Book XVIII, chap. xx.

1346. affiance. Faith, trust.

1418. he should die a holy man. Lancelot became a priest, and Guinevere an abbess.

THE HOLY GRAIL.

The legend of the Grail is bound up with the Arthurian story in all the early versions. The worship and search of the sacred chalice embodies the ardent religious feeling which in the middle ages went side by side, if not always hand in hand, with the joy of combat. The good knight prayed as vigorously as he fought or sinned. In Tennyson's account of the pursuit of the Grail by the knights of Arthur's Table Round, a glimpse, rather than a clear vision, is given of the strange blend of mystical yearning and hardy adventure which made up the code of chivalry.

A good many critics have tried to reduce this poem to a finished and consistent allegory. But it is a poem, not an argument. Much of the symbolism of the narrative may as well remain vague. Its merit lies in the intangible beauty of many passages, and in its general presentment of the everlasting struggle between human aspiration and human frailty.

According to the ancient story, the Holy Grail, which was the cup from which Christ drank at the Last Supper, was brought to Glastonbury in England by Joseph of Arimathea. In Malory's account, it is a descendant of Joseph who first brings the Grail into the story of Arthur and his knighthood.

2. Sir Percivale. Note that Sir Percivale and Sir Galahad are spoken of together in *Lancelot and Elaine*, 1256–1257. In the old German versions of the Grail story, Percivale, not Galahad, is hero. Wagner develops this theme in his great music-drama, *Parsival*.

15. puff'd the swaying branches into smoke. The pollen of the yew is so abundant that in a wind the effect of smoke is produced. Tennyson alludes to this again in *In Memoriam*, xxxix.: "With fruitful cloud and living smoke, Dark yew! . . ."

48. Aromat. Arimathea, home of the Joseph who placed the body of Christ in his own tomb. By the ancient tradition, Joseph had caught in the Grail the blood that flowed from Christ's side on the cross.

49. day of darkness. See Matthew, xxvii. 45.

52. Glastonbury . . . the winter thorn. "There is a variety of hawthorn which puts forth leaves and flowers about the time of Christmas. It is said to have originated at Glastonbury Abbey, and the original thorn was believed to have been the staff with which Joseph of Arimathea aided his steps on his wanderings from the Holy Land to Glastonbury, where he is said to have founded the celebrated Abbey. The first church, according to the legend, was ' built of wattles ' and interwoven twigs. In A.D. 439 St. Patrick is said to have visited the place, and to have founded the monastery, of which he became the abbot. In 542 King Arthur was buried there. The Abbey was several times repaired and rebuilt before the reign of Henry II, when it was destroyed by fire, and the large and splendid structure, the ruins of which still remain, was erected. It was the wealthiest abbey in England, except West-minster." So wrote Dr. W. J. Rolfe a quarter of a century ago. Very recently, extensive excavations have been made among the ruins at Glastonbury, and the tomb of Arthur is supposed to have been found.

61. Arviragus. According to legend, King of the Britons about 50 A.D.

66. miracle. Wonder, marvel. So in line 166 below.

67. to-day. In our time.

68. Here the story of the Grail and the Round Table begins. At this point, for convenience, may be given a summary of what follows:

68–165. Percivale, who is the principal speaker throughout, begins by telling how his sister, a saintly nun, dreamed of the legend that the Holy Grail should return again and heal the world. She describes to Percivale her vision of the Grail. Galahad, the purest of Arthur's knights, hears of her vision, goes to her, and is consecrated by her to the quest of the Grail.

166–360. In Arthur's Hall was the Siege Perilous, the Seat of Peril. There Galahad dared sit: whereupon came to all the Round Table the veiled glory of the Grail. Then all the knights are filled with zeal to seek the vanished Grail for a year and a day, and to strike to restore it to the clear vision of mankind, and so bring about a sort of Millenium. Arthur is absent at the moment, and, returning, is filled with doubt and dismay at this sudden scattering of his knights to "follow wandering fires." Their duty, he says, is

to stick to their knightly task as champions of the right.   But they
are under the glamour of the mystical vision; and they set forth,
each alone, to find the Grail.

361–457. Percivale tells the first part of his own adventures
in which it appears that he is in search of happiness first and holiness after, and therefore destined to fail in the Quest: " At first
he is over-confident (351–367); then unduly convicted of sins
(368–378); next he tries worship of beauty in nature (379–390),
then domestic love (391–400); then earthly splendor (401–420),
and popularity (421–439); each in turn fails to satisfy his thirst for
holiness, for each is essentially selfish (445–457).   Percivale fails
because he never forgets himself (456)" (Denney).

458–484. Galahad's part in the story.

485–539. Percivale and Galahad. The glorious passing of Galahad.

540–631. Percivale's hearer, the old monk Ambrosius, asks
" What about the other seekers for the Grail? "   Percivale, absorbed
in his own experience, goes on with his personal account.   Ambrosius repeats his question more clearly: " How about the rest of the
knights? " and at last Percivale begins to answer him.   He tells of
the adventure of Sir Bors, and sums up the experiences of the
others, as they related them to Arthur after their return (631–849).

850–916. The moral of the whole adventure is pointed, first by
Gawain and finally by Arthur.

110. use. Habit.

117–119. The painter Edwin Austin Abbey's Grail picture in the
Boston Public Library marvelously illustrates this passage.

138. so young youth. According to the old tale, Galahad was
but fifteen at the time of the Quest.

182–194. This is close to Malory's account; but notice how the
" good odors " and " meats and drinks " give an earthy touch to
the earlier narrative:

" And every knight sat in his own place as they were toforehand.
Then anon they heard cracking and crying of thunder, that them
thought that the place should all to-drive.   In the midst of this
blast entered a sunbeam more clearer by seven times than ever they
saw day, and all they were a-lighted with the grace of the Holy
Ghost   Then began every knight to behold other, and either

saw other by their seeming fairer than ever they saw afore. Not for then there was no knight might speak one word a great while, and so they looked every man on other, as they had been dumb. Then there entered into the hall the holy Grail covered with white samite, but there was none might see it, nor who bare it. And there was all the hall full filled with good odors, and every knight had such meats and drinks as he best loved in this world: and when the holy Graile had been borne through the hall, then the holy vessel departed suddenly, that they wist not where it became. Then had they all breath to speak. And then the king yielded thanking unto God of his good grace that he had sent them." Note that in this version of the story Arthur was present when the Grail appeared. Sir Gawain (not Percivale, as in Tennyson's tale) makes a sudden vow to seek for the Grail for a year and a day; the others catch the infection and leap to their feet and make the same vow before the King can protest. "Anon as king Arthur heard this he was greatly displeased, for he wist well that they might not against-say their vows. Alas! said king Arthur unto Sir Gawaine, ye have nigh slain me with the avow and the promise that ye have made. For through you ye have bereft me of the fairest fellowship and the truest knighthood that ever were seen together in any realm of the world."

224–257. This description of Camelot is parenthetic, and purely Tennysonian.

250. twelve great battles. See *Lancelot and Elaine*, 285.

297. a sign to maim. Destined to maim.

299. the King was hard. Percivale still believes the Grail-quest justified.

300. Taliessin. Most famous of British bards. The king uses his name symbolically, as he might have used " Apollo."

350. wyvern, lion, etc. The beasts, largely mythical, used in heraldic decoration.

454. her thou hast not known. That is, humility, mother of all virtues; see line 445 above.

456. thou hast not lost thyself. Percivale fails because it is his own glory or salvation he thinks of throughout his quest.

462. the sacring of the mass. The consecration of the bread and wine.

489–539. These lines describe the passing of Galahad — one of the most eloquent passages in the poem.

562. Came ye on none but phantoms, etc. Here Percivale's hearer returns to the question, "How about the other knights who went upon the Quest? What happened to them?" But Percivale is still absorbed in his own affair, and goes on to tell of how after his glimpse of the Grail, he lapsed into his old faults of selfishness.

630. Saw ye none beside? "I was asking about the *others*," Percivale's auditor reminds him.

646. his former madness. Malory represents Lancelot as going mad on one occasion, under the pressure of Guinevere's jealous anger; and as being cured, after some time, by the Holy Grail. See Malory, Book XI, chap. ix.; and Book XII, chap. IV.

661. Paynim amid their circles. Pagan in the midst of their magic circles of stone. The allusion is to the Druids and their relics, as at Stonehenge.

681. the seven clear stars of Arthur's Table Round. A British name for the constellation of the Great Bear, or the Big Dipper.

714–715. unicorns . . . basilisks . . . cockatrices. All fabulous creatures. The basilisk was a serpent that killed by its glance; the cockatrice another strange reptile monster: all frequently used in heraldic devices.

759. like him of Cana. See John, II, x.

777. Then I spake . . . holy saint. According to Malory Lancelot reveals his name to a hermit, who tells him that for all his fame as a knight, his sins have kept him from the Grail: "And for your presumption to take upon you in deadly sin for to be in His presence, where His flesh and His blood was, that caused you night not see it with worldly eyes . . . for your strength and manhood will not avail you and God be against you. . . .

"Then Sir Launcelot wept with heavy cheer, and said, Now I know well ye say me sooth. Sir, said the good man, hide none old sin from me. Truly, said Sir Launcelot, that were me full loth to discover. For this fourteen years I never discovered one thing that I have used, and that may I now blame my shame and my misadventure. And then he told there that good man all his life, and how he had loved a queen unmeasurably, and out of measure long; —

and all my great deeds of arms that I have done, I did the most part for the queen's sake, and for her sake would I do battle were it right or wrong, and never did I battle all only for God's sake, but for to win worship, and to cause me to be the better beloved, and little or nought I thanked God of it. Then Sir Launcelot said, I pray you counsel me. I will counsel you, said the hermit, if ye will ensure me that ye will never come in that queen's fellowship, as much as ye may forbear. And then Sir Launcelot promised him he would not, by the faith of his body." — Malory, Book XIII, chap. xx.

782–849. In this passage Tennyson greatly enlarges and embroiders the bare fabric of Malory's narrative, which runs as follows: —

" And the wind arose, and drove Launcelot more than a month throughout the sea, where he slept but little, but prayed to God that he might see some tidings of the Sancgreal. So it befell on a night, at midnight he arrived before a castle, on the back side, which was rich and fair. And there was a postern opened towards the sea, and was open without any keeping, save two lions kept the entry; and the moon shone clear. Anon Sir Launcelot heard a voice that said, Launcelot, go out of this ship, and enter into the castle, where thou shalt see a great part of thy desire. Then he ran to his arms, and so armed him, and so he went to the gate, and saw the lions. Then set he hand to his sword, and drew it. Then there came a dwarf suddenly, and smote him on the arm so sore that the sword fell out of his hand. Then heard he a voice say, Oh man of evil faith and poor belief, wherefore trowest thou more on thy harness than in thy Maker? for He might more avail thee than thine armour, in whose service thou art set. Then said Launcelot, Fair Father, Jesu Christ, I thank thee of thy great mercy, that thou reprovest me of my misdeed. Now see I well that ye hold me for your servant. Then took he again his sword, and put it up in his sheath, and made a cross in his forehead, and came to the lions, and they made semblant to do him harm. Notwithstanding he passed by them without hurt, and entered into the castle to the chief fortress, and there were they all at rest. Then Launcelot entered in so armed, for he found no gate nor door but it was open. And at the last he found a chamber whereof the door was shut, and he set his hand thereto to have opened it, but he might not." — Malory, Book XVII, chap. xiv.

862. deafer than the blue-eyed cat. The scientist Darwin discovered that pure white cats with blue eyes are usually deaf.

901. seeing that the King must guard that which he rules. Since it is the King's duty to care for his land and his people.

905. being done. When this work is done.

911. vision. Visionary, unreal.

912–914. And knows himself, etc. This may be paraphrased: "And knows that the essential or important part of himself is not unreal (though it is intangible); nor is God unreal, or Christ."

915. "I knew not what he meant." Percivale is of simple and rather limited intelligence, and the King's symbolism is beyond him.

THE PASSING OF ARTHUR.

In the poem *Morte d'Arthur*, published in 1842, Tennyson produced an earlier and much shorter version of this Idyll. The passage in Malory upon which the poem is mainly based must be given entire: —

"Therefore, said Arthur [unto Sir Bedivere], take thou Excalibur, my good sword, and go with it to yonder water side, and when thou comest there, I charge thee throw my sword in that water, and come again, and tell me what thou there seest. My lord, said Bedivere, your commandment shall be done, and lightly bring you word again. So Sir Bedivere departed, and by the way he beheld that noble sword, that the pommel and the haft was all of precious stones, and then he said to himself, if I throw this rich sword in the water, therefor shall never come good, but harm and loss. And then Sir Bedivere hid Excalibur under a tree. And so as soon as he might he came again unto the king, and said he had been at the water, and had thrown the sword into the water. What saw thou there? said the king. Sir, he said, I saw nothing but waves and winds. That is untruly said of thee, said the king; therefore go thou lightly again, and do my commandment; as thou art to me lief and dear, spare not, but throw it in. Then Sir Bedivere returned again, and took the sword in his hand; and then him thought sin and shame to throw away that noble sword; and so eft he hid the sword, and returned again, and told to the king that he had been at the water, and done his commandment. What saw thou there? said the king. Sir, he said, I saw nothing but the waters wappe and the waves wanne. Ah, traitor, untrue, said king Arthur, now hast thou betrayed me twice. Who would have weened that thou hast been to me so lief and dear, and thou art named a noble knight, and would betray me for the richness of the sword. But now go again lightly, for thy long tarrying putteth me in great jeopardy of my life, for I have taken cold. And but if thou do now as I bid thee, if ever I may see thee, I shall slay thee with mine own hands, for thou wouldst for my rich sword see me dead. Then Sir Bedivere departed, and went to the sword and lightly took it up, and went to the water side, and there he bound the girdle about the hilts, and then he threw the sword as far into the water as he might, and there came an arm and an hand above the water, and met it, and caught it, and so shook it thrice and brandished, and then vanished away the hand with the sword in the water. So Sir Bedivere came again to the king, and told him what he saw. Alas, said the king, help me hence, for I dread me I have tarried over long. Then Sir Bedivere took the king upon his back, and so went with him to that water side. And when they were at the water side, even fast by the bank hove a little barge, with many fair ladies in it, and among them all was a queen, and all they had black hoods, and all they wept and shrieked when they saw king Arthur. Now put me into the barge, said the king: and so he did softly; and there received him three queens with great mourning; and so they set them down. . . . Then Sir Bedivere cried: Ah my lord Arthur, what shall become of me now ye go from me and leave me here alone among mine enemies? Comfort thyself, said the king, and do as well as thou mayest, for in me is no trust for to trust in; for I will into the vale of Avilion to heal me of my grievous wound; and if thou hear never more of me, pray for my soul. But ever the queens and ladies wept and shrieked, that it was pity to hear. And as soon as Sir Bedivere had lost the sight of the barge, he wept and wailed, and so took the forest." — Malory, Book XXI, chap. v.

34. According to Malory, Gawain means his message for warning rather than for prophecy: " God hath sent me to you of his special grace, to give you warning that in no wise ye do battle us to-morn, but that ye take a treaty for a month day; and proffer

you largely, so as to-morn to be put in a delay. For within a month shall come Sir Launcelot with all his noble Knights, and rescue you worshipfully, and slay Sir Mordred, and all that ever will hold with him." (Malory, Book XXI, chap. iii.) In consequence Arthur tries to put off the struggle, and a truce is arranged with Mordred; but an accident brings the battle on, and Arthur is fatally wounded.

70. And shook him thro' the north. See *The Coming of Arthur,* line 511.

77. One lying in the dust at Almesbury. See *Guinevere.* At Almesbury occurred the final interview between the king and Guinevere, and there, according to Malory, she became nun, and finally Abbess.

81. Lyonnesse. The ancient land of Lyonnesse lay, according to fable, between Cornwall and the Scilly Islands.

90–91. when the great light of heaven Burned at his lowest. That is, on the shortest day of the year, late in December. The phases of the story correspond with the seasons, throughout.

105–110. Notice the irregular metrical structure of these lines. Can they be scanned?

153. Malory gives a very different account of the relationship between Arthur and Mordred. Upon that relationship, and not upon the episode of Launcelot and Guinevere, hangs the tragic motive of *Le Morte Darthur.*

164–169. In Malory, the battle is one of extermination. Arthur, Sir Bedivere, Sir Lucan, and Mordred are presently the only survivors. Sir Bedivere, remembering the warning of Gawain's ghost, tries to keep Arthur from attacking Mordred: " Tide me death, betide me life, saith the king, now I see him yonder alone he shall never escape mine hands, for at a better avail shall I never have him. God speed you well, said Sir Bedivere. Then the king gat his spear in both his hands, and ran toward Sir Mordred, crying: Traitor, now is thy death-day come. And when Sir Mordred heard Sir Arthur, he ran until him with his sword drawn in his hand. And there King Arthur smote Sir Mordred under the shield, with a foin of his spear, throughout the body, more than a fathom. And when Sir Mordred felt that he had his death wound he thrust himself with the might that he had up to the bur of King Arthur's spear. And right so he smote Arthur, with his sword holden in both his hands, on the side of the head, that the sword pierced the helmet and the brain-pan, and therewithal Sir Mordred fell stark dead to the earth; and the noble Arthur fell in a swoon to the earth, and there he swooned ofttimes." — Malory, Book XXI, chap. iv.

92. closed. Enclosed.

140. wastes. Lays waste.

170. So all day long, etc. With this line began Tennyson's early poem *Morte d'Arthur*, first published in 1842, but probably written in 1835, when the poet was but twenty-six and not long out of the university. So this was his first Arthurian poem, destined to be included in the Idyll which stands last in the series. The first *Morte d'Arthur* is to be found in *The Epic*, printed in the volume of 1842, *English Idylls and Other Poems*.

206. lightly. Swiftly.

244. For surer sign had follow'd. For some surer sign must or would have followed.

247. lief. Loved. . Compare German "Liebe".

254. chased. Engraved.

339. remorsefully. In the older sense: tenderly.

383. greaves and cuisses. Armor for the calves and thighs

440. And on the mere the wailing, etc. Here Tennyson's early poem *Morte d'Arthur* ends.

444. rhyme. Verse.

451. He comes again. See line 421 and Note, above.